What people are say

All My Love, Jesus

*I'm honored to recommend to you this wonderful new book, **All My Love, Jesus**, written by my dear friend, Rev. Ron Lambros. Through the years, Ron has chronicled his walk with God as he faced the issues of life that have brought him to this unique place of Christian service. I believe you will find hope and strength that will add to your journey, too.*

- Richard G. Lee, PhD, Founding Pastor,
First Redeemer Church, Cumming, GA

*For 40 years, my friend Ron Lambros has kept a journal of inspirational thoughts that God has given him in his time with the Lord. Ron is a man who walks with the Lord, and as you walk with him through **All My Love, Jesus**, your walk with the Lord will grow exponentially!*

- Dr. James Merritt, Speaker, Touching Lives Ministries, Inc.

*Scriptural, simple, personal, and powerful are words that best describe the devotional thoughts Ron Lambros has captured in **All My Love, Jesus**. I have known Ron for nearly forty years and each and every one of these daily thoughts are things Ron has lived and hammered out in his own walk with Jesus. I commend them to you, knowing the power is in the eternal truths of the Word of God, but believing the simplicity and practicality will make them readable and accessible to all.*

- Dr. Gary Hollingsworth, Executive Director-Treasurer,
South Carolina Baptist Convention

All My Love, Jesus

Personal Reminders
From the Heart of God

Ron Lambros

Published and printed in the United States of America.

Scriptures taken from the Holy Bible, New International Version®, NIV®. Copyright © 1973, 1978, 1984, 2011 by Biblica, Inc.™ Used by permission of Zondervan. All rights reserved worldwide. www.zondervan.com The "NIV" and "New International Version" are trademarks registered in the United States Patent and Trademark Office by Biblica, Inc.™

Scripture quotation marked The Message is taken from THE MESSAGE, copyright © 1993, 2002, 2018 by Eugene H. Peterson. Used by permission of NavPress. All rights reserved. Represented by Tyndale House Publishers, Inc.

ISBN: 978-0-578-47275-1

Dedication

All My Love, Jesus is dedicated to my sweet wife, Bridget, who loves me at my worst, comforts me in my deepest sorrow, makes me laugh when I feel like crying, and encourages me when I fear or falter. You make me believe in a wonderful God because I see Him in you every day. No man could love you more!

Forward

I am not a professional writer by trade. I have been in the ministry, serving in various capacities, for over 41 years. During that time, my Bible study and prayer life have grown and evolved as my spiritual life and understanding of God, His character, and His nature have grown and evolved.

I am a firm believer in the fact that God still speaks with, and to, people today, including me. No, I have never heard Him speak in an audible voice or in a burning bush, but I have heard Him speak through my study of His Word, in times of prayer, through godly counsel, and in the many sermons I have heard preached through the years.

Over more than 4 decades, I have learned that God is not a pie-in-the-sky kind of God. He is a personal God, who wants what's best for my life at all times. God has often spoken to me personally, guiding me with His wisdom, with His principles and precepts, and with His still, small voice when I faced challenging, uncertain, or difficult moments in my life. And when He did, I began to write down what He said in a personal journal, knowing I could go back to its pages when needed. Nothing has been more precious or dear to my heart than these notations and thoughts made in those special moments with our Heavenly Father.

I have often shared many of these journal entries with friends and family when I felt they could possibly benefit from my personal devotions that were so graciously inspired and given when I needed them most. Going one step further, I was asked to compile these devotions in book form for anyone and everyone to glean from. And thus, *All My Love, Jesus* was born.

This book is more than a labor of love. It is a collection of God's special moments with me through the years. The collection of devotions in this book are lovingly included with my prayer that the heart of those who read each one will be blessed with the same hope, strength, and encouragement I received as I wrote them.

I hope you enjoy the book! It was a joy to write because it reminded me all over again what a truly faithful, gracious, and loving God He really is.

How to Use This Devotional

When I set out to compile this devotional book, I wanted it to be different than any other I had ever personally seen, read, or used. So many of these devotionals are by dear friends or respected peers. They have blessed me tremendously and helped me grow spiritually. They encouraged me, gave me hope, joy and, sometimes, even brought tears. They are wonderful in their own right, but there are just so many devotionals on the market that I didn't want to follow suit. So I wrote this book.

All My Love, Jesus is *not* a *daily* devotional. It is, instead, a compilation of 250 devotions taken from my personal journal that can be read daily or depending on your need for that particular day. I truly desire the devotion you choose to meet your specific need at a specific time in your life.

With that in mind, you can read *All My Love, Jesus* in the following five ways:

1. Randomly: Simply pick up the book and read whatever page you choose;
2. By Title: Each devotion has a specific title. Look for one that intrigues you or sounds like it might be what you're looking for;
3. By Scripture: Each devotion is listed by the Bible text used for that particular devotion. If you know a text you love, or feel relates to your need, look up the page(s) and read away;

4. By Subject. I have listed 25 specific areas of need I feel are the key topics people deal with in their lives; things like anger, hope, faith, and God's will. Go to the content page and look up several devotions that deal specifically with what you need on that particular day or at that particular moment;
5. By Holiday: I have written specific devotions for most recognized holidays. On those particular days, I invite you to read that content-specific devotion.

Whichever way you choose, I hope each devotion you read is a source of hope, strength, and encouragement. Remember, it's not the words that you read that will help you, but it's the God of those words that will meet each and every need of your life! Enjoy the book!

Acknowledgements

Plans fail for lack of counsel,

but with many advisers they succeed.

- Proverbs 15:22

John Donne, the noted English poet and cleric, wrote, "No man is an island..." He knew that everyone is part of something much larger than themselves, and I agree. No matter the level of planning, talent, or giftedness, nothing is accomplished or satisfied on our own. Everything we are and do is a direct result of the experiences we encounter in our life's journey and the influence of hundreds, if not thousands, of people who have invested in us along the way.

All My Love, Jesus is no exception. While I may have spent the countless hours writing, compiling, and typing out this manuscript, I could not have written it without the help and encouragement of so many people, far too numerous to name here. But I do want to acknowledge and thank the following few who helped make this book go from a dream to a reality:

To my Lord and Savior, Jesus Christ, whose grace and mercy touch my soul at its deepest level. Thank you for caring enough to speak to me in your still, small voice, instructing and guiding my life for over four decades. You have given me life-changing material to write about, remember, and apply;

To my beloved wife and best friend, Bridget. You inspire me to write every day, if not with words, with my heart. Your constant encouragement drove me to finally put my soul to paper;

To Andrea Fuller, dear friend and gifted writer in her own right. Your eyes and heart saw the big picture and the smallest detail, and you made me a better writer with your wisdom and creativity;

To my 6th-grade teacher, Mrs. Lorena McGowan. You were the first to tell me that I had a gift and should use it. I finally did. I only wish you were alive to see it in print;

To so many family members and close friends who believe in me, pray for me, and support me as I continue in ministry, writing and seeking God's will for my life. There are far too many of you to list here, but I hope I have told you personally who you are, long before this book ever went to print;

And, finally, to you who are reading this book. My purpose in writing every word is to bring hope, strength, and encouragement into your life, just as I have found. They do not come from my words, but from the God who walks with me every day. I hope you discover more about Him through my efforts. All the glory and honor belong to Him!

Table of Contents

Trust Him with It All

Trust in the Lord with all your heart and lean not on your own understanding; in all your ways acknowledge him, and he will make your paths straight.
- Proverbs 3:5, 6

Faith is always tested at the intersection of "Why?" and "Trust Me!" We come to God with those situations and problems that make us ask Him "Why?" He answers with a simple "Trust Me!" You cannot trust God in those things which you choose and not trust Him in others. You either trust Him with it all or with nothing at all. Your choice will either provide you with a powerful faith to carry you through the ups and downs of life—or a faith that struggles with the slightest circumstance.

The choice is yours. Trust Him!

Take Him With You:

You either trust God with it all or with nothing at all.

Ron Lambros

Keys to Your Success

*I have hidden your word in my heart
that I might not sin against you.*
- Psalm 119:11

The strength and power needed to persevere in the Christian life are not revealed in moments of crisis by accident. They are nurtured in the quiet days of determined faith, Scripture reading, and private prayer. Then, when the moments of trial do come, we are prepared to react and overcome through the "training" which was done in secret.

Prepare your heart today for the trials that are just around the bend! Hold fast to your faith no matter the circumstance. Read God's Word daily and hide it in your heart for the days of testing. Pray earnestly, consistently, and thankfully.

These are the keys to your success in the Christian life.

Take Him With You:

Strength and power in the Christian life aren't by accident. They're developed.

That Person

First go and be reconciled to them;
then come and offer your gift.
- Matthew 5:24

We all have "that person" in our lives: the one who angers you just by the very mention of their name. God is clear that if we are to have fellowship with Him, we must first be reconciled to "that person." You may need to initiate the reconciliation, even if the issues aren't your fault.

You know who "that person" is, and God is telling you to repair that relationship right now. It may hurt your pride a bit, but it will bless the heart of God—and He, in turn, will bless yours!

Take Him With You:

God wants you to be reconciled to "that person".

Ron Lambros

Do Great Things for God

The LORD does not look at the things people look at.
People look at the outward appearance,
but the LORD looks at the heart.
- I Samuel 16:7

Too many people suffer from low spiritual self-esteem. They feel unfit or unable to make a difference in the Kingdom of God. Satan wants us to feel that we can't do the work God has called us to do.

Fight that impulse, and humbly challenge yourself to do great things for God! If you are empowered by the Holy Spirit, you can accomplish anything! Man may look at the outward appearance, but God looks at the heart! You matter to God and your life counts, so do something for Him today, whether it's large or small.

It will make a difference!

Take Him With You:

The Holy Spirit can help you
accomplish anything for God.

He Knows What He's Doing

But I trust in you, LORD; I say, "You are my God."
- Psalm 31:14

Do you really trust God? God is not a spiritual vending machine where you insert your prayer, push a button, and receive an answer, and if you don't like that answer, you insert more prayers and keep pushing buttons until you get the answer that you want. That's not God! If your prayer is made with faith, trust, and thanksgiving, He'll give you the right answer the very first time. Trust me! He knows what He's doing!

Take Him With You:

God always gives you the right answer to your prayer.

God's Answers to Life's Trials

Come to me, all you who are weary and burdened,
and I will give you rest.
- Matthew 11:28

Weariness. That feeling we often face at the end of far too many days. Life simply saps us of our energy and strength. Marriage problems. Prodigal child. Financial burdens. An unfaithful spouse. Sickness. An anxious spirit. Soon, all energy is gone, and we slump over into an emotional heap.

God says for all of us who are weary to simply come to Him and He will give us rest. R-E-S-T. God's answer for life's trials. And all we have to do is come.

Take Him With You:

If you come to Him, God will give you rest.

More Than We Deserve

But because of his great love for us,
God, who is rich in mercy...
- Ephesians 2:4

When was the last time you stopped to thank God for what you DO have rather than complain to Him about what you DON'T have? If we pause and search our hearts, we will see and admit that God has blessed each of us far more than we deserve.

After all, after salvation, everything else is a bonus.

God gave us His best and His fullest at Calvary. Let THAT be the contentment of your heart today!

Take Him With You:

Let Calvary be the contentment of your heart.

Ron Lambros

Never Give Up

The Lord is not slow in keeping his promise,
as some understand slowness. Instead he is patient with
you, not wanting anyone to perish,
but everyone to come to repentance.
- 2 Peter 3:9

We serve an incredibly awesome and faithful God! After praying for him for 32 years, my 92-year-old father prayed to receive Jesus Christ as his Lord and Savior last night! Dad was the first person I shared Christ with after my own salvation. My family has been praying for him for so many years, and God has honored us in an unbelievable way!

Stand firm in your prayers for anything and anyone, and never give up! God is so faithful! Burdens are truly lifted at Calvary!

Take Him With You:

Keep praying and never give up!

Become a Living Testimony

Therefore, I urge you, brothers and sisters, in view of God's mercy, to offer your bodies as a living sacrifice, holy and pleasing to God—this is your true and proper worship.
- Romans 12:1

There is a huge misconception in the Christian life that God is only interested in what we do for Him. While these acts may be done with the best of intentions, God is far more interested in what we BECOME as believers than in what we DO!

If we spend more time reading His Word, growing in faith, learning more about Him daily, and worshipping Him as we should, our lives will become living testimonies of His grace, mercy, and power, and our impact on those around us will be far greater as we live each day of our lives!

Take Him With You:

What you become is more important than what you do.

Ron Lambros

Trust the Shepherd

When he has brought out all his own, he goes on ahead of them, and his sheep follow him because they know his voice.
- John 10:4

Life doesn't come with a GPS, but it does come with a Shepherd. When we come to our forks in the road, when we seek answers to questions we alone can't answer, when we don't understand why we're going through what we're going through, we, like sheep, must simply trust the Shepherd and follow His voice. He will lead us beside the still waters of peace as He assumes the responsibility for our every care.

Take Him With You:

Always trust God and follow His lead.

He Understands

...being found in appearance as a man,
he humbled himself...
- Philippians 2:8

Think that you have a problem that God just doesn't understand?

Consider this:

The tongue that raised Lazarus from the dead was often parched.

The hands that healed the blind and leprous had dirty fingernails.

The feet that walked to Calvary were blistered and calloused.

Jesus was just like you and me. He lived, breathed, and hungered. He was often tired, thirsty, and discouraged. And because of that, He understands exactly what you're going through!

Take Him With You:

God understands exactly what you're going through.

Ron Lambros

God Uses the Ordinary

But God chose the foolish things of the world to shame the wise; God chose the weak things of the world to shame the strong.
- I Corinthians 1:27

God has always been so good about doing extraordinary things using ordinary people:

- a shepherd with a sling and a staff

- a Nazarite with a jawbone

- a peasant woman with an alabaster box

- a harlot with a simple rope.

God knows something we need to learn: it's not our abilities that matter to Him—it's that we make ourselves available to Him. When we do, He does the extraordinary through us.

Never sell yourself short! You matter and have unbelievable potential in the hands of a sovereign God!

Take Him With You:

You have unbelievable potential to God.

In the Beginning

In the beginning God...
- Genesis 1:1

The Bible begins with, "*In the beginning God...*" These are not mere words, but they also show God's character. In the beginning of EVERYTHING, God is there! When the first cancer cell is found, with the phone's first ring, with the first revelation of an unfaithful spouse, with the first sign of impending layoffs, with the first feelings of doubt or fear...in each of these and every other circumstance or crisis in your life, God is there.

And if He is there with you in the beginning, He promises to be there with you to the end!

Take Him With You:

God is with you from the very beginning.

Ron Lambros

"*IT*"

So I say, walk by the Spirit, and you will not
gratify the desires of the flesh.
- Galatians 5:16

We all have an "IT" in our lives. "IT" is that thing you promise God that you'll never, ever do again: that sin, that doubt, that fear, that guilt, that anger, that worry...that "IT"...but you do "IT" anyway.

God is in the "IT" business and is waiting to help you overcome "IT" and forgive you when you do "IT." He won't hold "IT" against you or ever deny you forgiveness.

Give "IT" to Him right now and live your life free from your weight of "IT" today!

Take Him With You:

God wants your "IT".

After All That

Jesus replied,
"What is impossible with man is possible with God."
- Luke 18:27

Let's see: Day 1, created light and dark; Day 2, created sky; Day 3, created land, sea, and vegetation; Day 4, created sun, moon, and stars; Day 5, created birds and all sea creatures; Day 6, created all land animals, taking special time to create man and woman; Day 7, He rested.

Now, after all that, do you really think that your problem is too big for Him to handle?

Take Him With You:

God can handle your biggest problem.

Ron Lambros

That Same God

Whether you turn to the right or to the left, your ears will hear a voice behind you, saying, "This is the way; walk in it."
- Isaiah 30:21

God has asked each of us to take a journey called life. For some, the journey is pleasant and fulfilling; for others, it is painful and sorrowful. The key to remember is that the same loving God is in both journeys, every step of the way, quietly guiding, encouraging, and strengthening us for what lies ahead.

God's roadmap is before you today, and He is your biggest cheerleader! "*This is the way; walk in it!*"

Take Him With You:

God has provided a perfect path for you to follow.

God Intends It for Good

You intended to harm me, but God intended it for good...
- Genesis 50:20

God's greatest blessings are sometimes dressed as trials, tests, and suffering. Sometimes these circumstances are of our own making; sometimes, they're the result of others' actions for which we have no control. However, nothing happens in the life of a child of God that He does not allow, so He can use even the most difficult situation to bless us.

Remember, what man often intends for evil, God intends for good!

Take Him With You:

God can make a blessing out of your most difficult situation or circumstance.

Ron Lambros

A Pat on the Back

The LORD your God is with you, the Mighty Warrior who saves, He will take great delight in you; in his love he will no longer rebuke you, but will rejoice over you with singing.
- Zephaniah 3:17

We all need encouragement from time to time—that pat on the back that lets us know that we're loved, wanted, and appreciated.

Have you ever stopped to consider that's exactly what the cross is doing? On the cross, Jesus Christ, the very Son of God, is telling you and me that He'd rather die for us than live without us. Now THAT'S a pat on the back!

Take Him With You:

Jesus would rather die for you than live without you.

The Eyes of Faith

So we fix our eyes not on what is seen,
but on what is unseen, since what is seen is temporary,
but what is unseen is eternal.
- II Corinthians 4:18

Looking out my office window this morning, I saw a sparrow perched on a branch. Suddenly, my mind was flooded with song: *Why should I be discouraged? Why should the shadows come? Why should my heart feel lonely? When Jesus is my portion, a constant friend is He. His eye is on the sparrow, and I know He watches me!* (Civilla Martin) God makes Himself known in the most uncommon and unusual ways, but you must look for Him with the eyes of faith to recognize Him!

Take Him With You:

To really see God,
you must look for Him with the eyes of faith.

Ron Lambros

Let Your Anchor Hold

Praise be to the God and Father of our Lord Jesus Christ,
the Father of compassion and the God of all comfort...
- II Corinthians 1:3

There are dark days in the life of every believer—days of fear, doubt, grief, and discouragement. In those days, we should seek our Abba Father, our Heavenly Daddy, who says to cast our cares on Him, and promises that, even in the midst of our deepest despair, He will never leave us or forsake us and will always work things out for our good!

Let your anchor hold tight to these promises and to His faithfulness, and find comfort in Him during your times of anguish and uncertainty.

Take Him With You:

Anchor your faith to God's promises.

Salt and Light

You are the salt of the earth...
You are the light of the world.
- Matthew 5:13, 14

I was recently asked, "If your church shut its doors today, would your community know it?" Thinking about this, I took it a step further: If God took me home today, would anyone really notice that I was gone? Would my life's end truly have an impact? If not, I'm not being the salt and light that I'm called to be. I want to make a difference. I want to leave a Godly legacy and heritage. I want my life to count! Do you?

Take Him With You:

God wants you to make a difference.

Ron Lambros

Stretch Your Faith

And without faith it is impossible to please God, because anyone who comes to him must believe that he exists and that he rewards those who earnestly seek him.
- Hebrews 11:6

As the leader of a ministry, I must faithfully guard against mediocrity, complacency, and being satisfied with the status quo. *Average* can be a death-knell to any ministry AND to the Christian life in general. Each day, we need to challenge ourselves to do even greater things for God, to stretch our faith, and to mature in our understanding of His ways. When we do this, God will do amazing things through our lives.

Take Him With You:

Challenge yourself daily to do greater things for God.

The Crunching of the Apple

Greater love has no one than this:
to lay down one's life for one's friend.
- John 15:13

The cross was always God's idea, and Jesus freely came for that specific purpose. Best-selling author, Max Lucado, makes an incredible statement about God's plan and love for us through the cross when he says, "*Even while the crunching of the apple was still sounding in the garden, Jesus was leaving for Calvary.*"

What an awesome thought, and what an even more awesome God!

Take Him With You:
The cross was always God's idea.

Ron Lambros

Forgive Yourself

So if the Son sets you free, you will be free indeed.
- John 8:36

All of us know that we must forgive others if we, ourselves, desire to be forgiven. But we often overlook the necessity (and joy) of forgiving the one person who often needs it the most: ourselves. Stop beating yourself up for past mistakes or failures. Seek God's forgiveness first, and then do yourself a favor and forgive yourself. Never carry the burden of yesterday's mistakes into today or allow it to mask the promise of tomorrow. Cut yourself some slack and just forgive yourself!

Take Him With You:

Forgiving yourself is just as important as forgiving others.

God Cheers Us On

Jesus looked at them and said,
"With man this is impossible, but not with God;
all things are possible with God."
- Mark 10:27

God builds each one of our dreams with His bricks of the impossible. While we often limit ourselves with our own doubts, fears, and insecurities, God cheers us on to do bigger and greater things with our life.

Never dream too small or let the world convince you that it can't be done or that you can't do it. Nothing is impossible with God, but apart from Him, we can do nothing!

Take Him With You:

God can help your biggest dreams come true.

Ron Lambros

Tears

Record my misery; list my tears on your scroll—
are they not in your record?
- Psalm 56:8

There is a quiet catharsis to tears. They purge and cleanse our spirits and speak to God as no words can. Many tears fall from the eyes while many fall unseen from the heart. Either way, God catches each one, from the quiet sighs to the rivers of grief, and places them in a bottle. In this way, He shares your every prayer, need, or unspoken anguish, and His tears flow freely with yours.

Take Him With You:

God understands your tears.

God's Assurance

The LORD will guide you always; he will satisfy your needs
in a sun-scorched land and will strengthen your frame.
You will be like a well-watered garden,
like a spring whose waters never fail.
- Isaiah 58:11

Read the story of God's conversation with Noah. God told him just how tall, how wide, and how long to build the ark, but not once did God ever mention putting a keel on it! That was God's assurance to Noah, and to each of us, that if we obey God and follow His instructions, we can weather the floods that come into our lives when we leave the steering and guidance with Him!

Take Him With You:

God will guide your life when you leave the destination to Him.

Ron Lambros

No Will of Your Own

Do not conform to the pattern of this world, but be transformed by the renewing of your mind. Then you will be able to test and approve what God's will is— his good, pleasing and perfect will.
- Romans 12:2

It is sometimes difficult to understand when God asks you to do something so extraordinary or different than you've ever done before. You set your course, and God changes it. What to do? The lesson is simple: obedience is better than sacrifice, and you will never experience the complete and total will of God for your life until you have absolutely no will of your own.

Give your life, with all of its hopes and dreams, to Him. He will direct you in the way you should go, and He always knows what's best!

.

Take Him With You:

You will never truly know God's will until you surrender your own will to Him.

God's Bigger Perspective

"For My thoughts are not your thoughts, nor are your ways My ways," declares the Lord. "For as the heavens are higher than the earth, so are My ways higher than your ways and my thoughts than your thoughts."
- Isaiah 55:8, 9

If we're honest, there are times when we feel that God has forsaken us. Life, with all its trials, takes its toll on our emotions and spiritual balance. It is at those very moments when God speaks softly and asks each of us to stand firm, believing that all of His promises to us are true, though we don't always understand what He is doing.

God always has a bigger perspective than the finite problem we are facing.

Take Him With You:

God's perspective is always bigger than yours.

Ron Lambros

Be Yourself

But you are a chosen people, a royal priesthood, a holy nation, God's special possession, that you may declare the praises of him who called you out of darkness into his wonderful light.
- I Peter 2:9

Many of us get frustrated and discouraged because we want to be something God did not create us to be. We would all be a lot happier if we were to use the skills, talents, and gifts God gave each of us to the very best of our abilities, to bring Him honor, glory, and praise every day, instead of trying to be something or someone we're not.

There is only one you.

You are unique and special in God's eyes. He created you to be you and no one else, so be the best you that you can possibly be! You'll be much happier and far more fulfilled, and God will be more pleased and blessed by all you do!

Take Him With You:

Be the person God created you to be.

God Steps In

Cast all your anxiety on him because he cares for you.
- I Peter 5:7

God must have a great deal of patience with us, and life often proves it. How many times have we worried, fretted, or lost sleep over a situation—then, when we finally gave up trying to solve our dilemma in our own strength, God steps in, solves the problem, and then asks why we were worried in the first place? All too often, we have to come to the end of ourselves before God will do anything!

Why waste the energy? Give Him your cares and concerns, and let Him carry the load for you. He loves to do it, and being free of that weight sure makes life easier and the journey more enjoyable!

Take Him With You:

God will carry your heaviest load if you let Him.

Ron Lambros

A Single Drop of Water

I will give you a new heart and put a new spirit in you;
I will remove from you your heart of stone
and give you a heart of flesh.
- Ezekiel 36:26

We all know people who are seemingly unreachable with the Gospel. We have shared and prayed for their salvation with no apparent success. Today, I was reminded that the Gospel can be like a single drop of water: seemingly small and insignificant at first, yet slowly, surely, with time, that single drop of water can wear away even the hardest stone. So stay faithful in sharing your faith, and you will see God's ability to save even the hardest sinner!

Take Him With You:

Stay faithful in sharing your faith.

God's Timing

But those who hope in the LORD will renew their strength.
They will soar on wings like eagles; they will run and not
grow weary, they will walk and not be faint.
- Isaiah 40:31

Why do we fret and worry and sometimes question if God will answer our prayers when we need them? Remember, prayer is something we do in our time; answering prayers is something God does in His.

If you're struggling with the wait, remember that it wasn't until Abraham lifted the knife over Isaac that God provided the substitute ram for the sacrifice. It may be the 11th hour, but if you're faithful, God will answer your prayers, and always in a way and at the time that has His glory and your best interest at heart!

Take Him With You:

God will answer your prayers at the right time.

Ron Lambros

Be Still

He says, "Be still, and know that I am God; I will be exalted among the nations, I will be exalted in the earth."
- Psalm 46:10

Why is it that we often feel that we have to help God do something in our lives? He gives us His plan, His purpose, and His promise that He'll do something, but we have a better idea and muddy up the waters. Abraham and Sarah had a better idea because they grew impatient and didn't want to wait for God to fulfill the promise He made to them. Look at the trouble it caused, even to this very day!

It's always best to heed God's Word, *"Be still, and know that I am God"* (emphasis on "I")! God's ways are so much higher and greater than ours, and we cannot even begin to comprehend the depth of His wisdom!

Trust God, be patient, and let Him fulfill His promises in your life! He will get the glory, and you will get a life filled with joy and satisfaction as He works out His perfect plan and purpose for your life!

Take Him With You:
God has everything under control and He doesn't need your help.

Focus on God

Since, then, you have been raised with Christ,
set your hearts on things above, where Christ is,
seated at the right hand of God.
- Colossians 3:1

I am thoroughly convinced that there are people who cross our paths every day that do nothing but discourage us and make us lose focus on the big picture of what God has called us to do. If we allow them, they will steal our joy, our enthusiasm, and our calling.

When you come across people like that, give them no time or opportunity. God is the source of our joy, and we must spend our energies focused on Him alone.

Take Him With You:

Spend your energy focusing on God.

Ron Lambros

When All Hell Breaks Loose

Do not let your hearts be troubled.
You believe in God; believe also in me.
- John 14:1

There are so many problems that can trouble us these days: financial pressure, job loss, illness, wayward children, broken marriages, compromised trust. We often ask, "Where is God when all hell breaks loose in my life?" The answer is very simple: He's right where He's always been...walking beside you through every difficulty and heartache you may be facing.

Today, above the thunder of every storm, hear His words of comfort: *"Let not your hearts be troubled! Trust in Me!"*

Take Him With You:

God is with you in every storm.

Only Today Matters

Therefore do not worry about tomorrow, for tomorrow will worry about itself. Each day has enough trouble of its own.
- Matthew 6:34

There are three words you need to tell yourself every day: "Only today matters!" Yesterday is gone and can never be repeated, and tomorrow is completely out of your control. So ask God to give you the wisdom and discernment for today only, release His power of forgiveness for your yesterdays, and ask Him to handle your tomorrows. Today is all you need to be concerned with, and what you do today will pave the way for everything that follows.

Take Him With You:

Ask God to simply help you take care of today.

Ron Lambros

Burdens

Praise be to the Lord, to God our Savior, who daily bears our burdens. Our God is a God who saves...
- Psalm 68:19, 20

Why do we often carry the heavy burdens that God wants to carry for us? Do we think they're too big for Him to handle or too small for Him to care about? He has lovingly told us to cast ALL our cares on Him, and if He can bear the weight of all the sin of the world in the form of a Roman cross, I know He can carry the weight of your personal and private cares.

Give Him your every care and concern today. His shoulders are broad enough and strong enough to bear your biggest burden, and His heart is big enough to be concerned with your smallest care!

Take Him With You:

Big or small, cast all of your cares on Him.

Mustard Seed Moments

He replied, "Because you have so little faith. Truly I tell you, if you have faith as small as a mustard seed, you can say to this mountain, 'Move from here to there,' and it will move. Nothing will be impossible for you."
- Matthew 17:20

Ever have a "mustard seed moment?" Many times in our lives, we allow circumstances and trials to overshadow our faith in God and His promises. Scripture tells us that our faith, even when incredibly small, can overcome even the most difficult situation, obstacle, or circumstance, no matter how hopeless it may seem.

Hold on to your faith, even if it's no bigger than a mustard seed, and God will see you through every challenge. God will always show Himself strong on your behalf, and He never fails!

Take Him With You:

Hold on to your faith, no matter how small it may be.

Ron Lambros

Opening Our Prison Doors

...because through Christ Jesus the law of the Spirit who gives life has set you free from the law of sin and death.
- Romans 8:2

Most of us have never been incarcerated, but many of us are jailed every day, held fast behind the iron bars of fear, doubt, worry, anger, unforgiveness, and a myriad of other emotional hardships. We yearn to be free, but we struggle when we attempt to gain that freedom on our own, failing miserably time and time again.

God can do what we cannot do. He can free us from the bonds and slavery of our emotional unrest. Simply ask Him to help you to remain steadfast in your faith, and then watch your prison doors swing open wide!

Take Him With You:

God can free you from the prison of your emotions.

God's Filter

Finally, brothers and sisters, whatever is true, whatever is noble, whatever is right, whatever is pure, whatever is lovely, whatever is admirable—if anything is excellent or praiseworthy—think about such things.
- Philippians 4:8

Every moment of every day, our minds are bombarded with hundreds of thousands of messages, all competing for our attention and our spiritual or emotional responses. How do you separate the important from the frivolous? Philippians 4:8: "*Whatever things are true, honest, just, pure, lovely, of a good report; if there be any virtue, any praise, think on these things.*" That's God's filter for proper thinking.

Makes choosing our priorities easier, doesn't it?

Take Him With You:

Let God's filter guide your thinking.

Blessing God

I have brought you glory on earth
by finishing the work you gave me to do.
- John 17:4

"I have brought you glory on earth by finishing the work you gave me to do." - John 17:4 (NIV). There is great joy, peace, and satisfaction in this verse. If you faithfully accomplish this result and can honestly make this statement from your heart after any season in your life, you have been successful, and have blessed the heart of God.

Take Him With You:

Blessing God is a mark of true success in your life.

Always Remember

Taste and see that the Lord is good;
blessed is the one who takes refuge in him.
- Psalm 34:8

A word for today and every day: God is still God, and God is still good!

Take Him With You:

God is still God, and God is still good!

Ron Lambros

Ready for the Day

In the morning, Lord, you hear my voice; in the morning I lay my requests before you and wait expectantly.
- Psalm 5:3

Looking out as a new day begins, filled with opportunities and hope.

I don't know everything today holds, but I'm sure of these things: God's mercies are new to me once again, He is sovereign, He's on the throne, and no matter how I feel or what circumstances or challenges might arise, God is still in control.

Yep, I'm ready for the day!

Take Him With You:

Begin each day by reminding yourself that God hasn't changed!

Be Amazed!

And they were all amazed at the greatness of God.
- Luke 9:43

My wish for each of us is that we never lose our amazement at the wonders of God. His Word tells us that we are to be like little children if we are to understand and appreciate His ways. What child is never amazed or filled with wonder? God's unconditional love, His unfailing promises, and the hope of life with Him forever should cause each of us to pause and be amazed every day.

Hallelujah! What a Savior!

Take Him With You:

Never lose your amazement at the wonders of God!

Ron Lambros

You're Never Alone

Have I not commanded you? Be strong and courageous.
Do not be afraid; do not be discouraged,
for the Lord your God will be with you wherever you go.
- Joshua 1:9

Feeling alone or abandoned? Nature sings a symphony of God's presence every moment of the day, from the blue of the sky to the songbird's warble; from the brush of the wind on your face to the cooing of a baby; from the heart beating within your chest to the twinkling of a star's light in the evening sky, they all remind us that He is always with us. And because He is with us, He hears our every cry and every prayer.

You're never alone! God is always there!

Take Him With You:
All nature sings a symphony of God's presence!

The Irresistible Force

Jesus Christ is the same yesterday and today and forever.
- Hebrews 13:8

Faith and trust are at the core of a personal relationship with God. Without them, that relationship cannot exist. Life brings challenges and trials that will test them both, but never forget that we serve an unchanging, unfailing God. The ebb-and-flow of life, with all of its challenges and cares, will always be met head-on by the irresistible force of a loving and compassionate God who always has your best interest at heart.

Take Him With You:

We serve an unchanging, unfailing God.

Ron Lambros

Never Be Blinded

When you pass through the waters, I will be with you;
and when you pass through the rivers,
they will not sweep over you.
When you walk through the fire, you will not be burned;
the flames will not set you ablaze.
- Isaiah 43:2

Too often, our faith lies battered and bloodied on the battlefield of daily living. Our personal crises, trails, tests, and fears often cause us to lose sight of the fact that God is always with us, He loves us unconditionally, and He never changes.

Never be blinded by your circumstances or fear. God is above each and every trial you are facing, and He will bring you through each one if you stay faithful and trust in Him.

Take Him With You:

Never be blinded by your circumstances or fear.

Miracles

I am the Lord, the God of all mankind.
Is anything too hard for me?
- Jeremiah 32:27

With every trial and test, we must ask, "Is anything too hard for God?" How we answer that question will shed light on the depth of our faith. The patriarchs of old don't have a corner on the "miracle market." God still performs His miracles every day, but we often let our fear and doubt blind us from seeing them.

Stay strong and believe no matter your circumstance. There's nothing too hard for Him to handle!

Take Him With You:

There's nothing too hard for God!

Ron Lambros

The Big Picture

He has made everything beautiful in its time.
He has also set eternity in the human heart; yet no one can
fathom what God has done from beginning to end.
- Ecclesiastes 3:11

Discouragement and disappointment often occur when we view our lives through the limits of the here-and-now and not through the eyes of faith. God always knows the beginning from the end, and everything in-between. His ways surpass our own, and He knows what will happen in the future, as opposed to just the immediate. God always sees the "big picture" of our lives, and what we sometimes perceive as a negative is often God's blessing in disguise.

Take Him With You:

Your biggest challenges and difficulties are often God's blessings in disguise.

God is Always There

Be strong and courageous. Do not be afraid or terrified because of them, for the Lord your God goes with you; he will never leave you nor forsake you.
- Deuteronomy 31:6

If we're honest, we often feel alone and isolated, forced to face our trials and circumstances with no one to help us. We feel abandoned by friends, family, and sometimes, even God Himself.

When facing your moments of loneliness and feelings of isolation, remember the words of Christ as they echo through your heart: "*I will never leave you or forsake you*" and "*I am with you always.*"

You're never alone in any situation or circumstance! God is always there!

Take Him With You:

**God is always with you in
every situation or circumstance.**

Ron Lambros

When You Don't Understand

Great is our Lord and mighty in power;
his understanding has no limit.
- Psalm 147:5

As we go through the daily grind of life, we often face situations that we simply don't understand. Our minds cannot comprehend how a loving God could allow some tragedies or heart-breaking situations to occur.

These are the defining moments of our faith because God is challenging us to trust Him when our hearts don't understand. It's okay to ask, "Why?" Just remember that He always knows what He's doing.

Never doubt or fear. Simply trust Him!

Take Him With You:

Trust God even when you don't understand.

When Storms Come

He got up, rebuked the wind and said to the waves,
"Quiet! Be still!"
Then the wind died down and it was completely calm.
- Mark 4:39

The storms and tempests of life come in all shapes and sizes, with varying degrees of intensity. And no one is immune to them. They always come.

Often during these unsettling storms, our spirits become restless, fearful, and anxious, and our faith flounders as the waves of doubt and fear crash within our lives. At that moment, we must determine to trust in the One who can calm the stormiest of times with His simple words, *"Peace, be still!"*

Never forget, the wind and the waves still know His name and they still obey Him!

Take Him With You:

God can calm any storm in your life.

Ron Lambros

Idols

Do not worship any other god,
for the Lord, whose name is Jealous, is a jealous God.
- Exodus 34:14

Many times in our Christian life, we lose focus. Our prayers seem to go unanswered, and God seems so far away. We will experience these unsettling feelings when we put other things—idols—before God, the idols of our own choosing: our career, time, friends, family...things. They can all seem innocent enough on their own, but they're wrong when we make them our priority over God! God is a jealous God and will not allow any other gods before Him!

Do you want the power back in your spiritual life? Then determine who or what you are really worshiping!

Take Him With You:

God will not allow you to have
any other gods before Him.

-54-

Regrets

Brothers and sisters, I do not consider myself yet to have taken hold of it. But one thing I do: Forgetting what is behind and straining toward what is ahead, I press on toward the goal to win the prize for which God has called me heavenward in Christ Jesus.
- Philippians 3:13, 14

John Greenleaf Whittier once wrote, "*For all sad words of tongue and pen, The saddest are these, 'It might have been.'*"

We all regret past mistakes and lost opportunities, but our God is a God of the here-and-now, and we can start again right where we are. God wants you to forget what you can't control and concentrate on what you have yet to accomplish! If done for His glory, you're sure to succeed!

Take Him With You:

You can start over right where you are.

Ron Lambros

Just Be You

*I praise you because I am fearfully and wonderfully made;
your works are wonderful, I know that full well.
- Psalm 139:14*

I believe that much of the unhappiness and frustration we often encounter in our Christian journey stems from our desire to be something or someone God did not create us to be. Each of us was *"fearfully and wonderfully made,"* empowered by Almighty God with gifts and talents specific to what He desires for our lives. Live out the life you were created for and watch how God blesses and empowers it!

Take Him With You:

Live the life you were created for.

Faith Believes

Let us hold unswervingly to the hope we profess,
for he who promised is faithful.
- Hebrews 10:23

Sometimes, even with all our prayers and pleading, the spouse still leaves, the marriage fails, the child becomes a prodigal, the deal falls through, a job is lost, a loved one dies...and we get angry and bitter toward God because He didn't answer our prayers the way we wanted Him to. Faith believes even when prayers go unanswered and grows when we put the results of our praying in His hands. He's always faithful and never fails. Trust Him!

Take Him With You:

Trust God no matter how He answers your prayers.

Ron Lambros

A Matter of the Will

And when you stand praying, if you hold anything against anyone, forgive them, so that your Father in heaven may forgive you your sins.
- Mark 11:25

The Lord commands us to "*Love one another.*" That kind of love is a sign of true discipleship. But many of us have people in our lives that we feel aren't worthy of or don't deserve our love because they have betrayed us or hurt us in an incredible way.

Our hurt and betrayal, while personally painful, doesn't alter the fact that we are to love even "our enemies." We must realize that love is a matter of the will, not of the heart, and with God's help, we can will to love, and to forgive, anyone for anything!

Always remember, Jesus Himself forgave Judas and each of us before going to the cross, and while we were yet sinners, He died for us.

Now that's love!

Take Him With You:
God can help you forgive anyone for anything.

Master Moments

"Do I not fill heaven and earth?" declares the Lord.
- Jeremiah 23:24

Enjoy your "Master moments" each day, the little things God does or brings into your life to remind you that He's always there, He's always in control, and that everything will work out. Special moments like the laughter of your grandchildren playing in the backyard, His palette of colors at sunset, a hug from a loving spouse, the soft feel of a spring breeze on your face. All of these, and thousands more, remind us every day of His sovereignty and presence. Enjoy each one as a gift and as a reminder that He loves you, He's always with you, and He cares about your every need.

Take Him With You:

God reminds you every day of His love, sovereignty, and presence.

God's Guarantee

For I am convinced that neither death nor life, neither angels nor demons, neither the present nor the future, nor any powers, neither height nor depth, nor anything else in all creation, will be able to separate us from the love of God that is in Christ Jesus our Lord.
- Romans 8:38, 39

Guarantees. You get them with everything from your automobile to your computer and cell phone. Sadly, most aren't worth the paper they're written on because they're filled with limitations, conditions, restrictions, and exemptions.

But King David reminds us of one guarantee that we can always believe in. We're guaranteed that nothing, *NOTHING*, can ever separate us from the love of God! No blunder, no slip-up, no failure, no circumstance...we can do absolutely nothing to quench the unconditional love of Almighty God for each of us.

Now that's a guarantee!

Take Him With You:

There is nothing that can separate you from God's love...nothing!

His Answer Will Come

Before they call I will answer;
while they are still speaking I will hear.
- Isaiah 65:24

Is your back against the wall? You feel that today is the day your prayer MUST be answered? The money's needed. The job must come through. The healing must take place. The situation must be corrected. We have to remember that God doesn't answer our prayers with earthly logic or limits. He answers with unlimited wisdom and unconditional love.

Pray in faith, believing, then wait for His answer. It WILL come, and ALWAYS when it should.

Take Him With You:

God doesn't answer your prayers with earthly logic or limits.

Ron Lambros

No Earthly Burden

Cast your cares on the Lord and he will sustain you;
He will never let the righteous be shaken.
- Psalm 55:22

Burdens. We all have them. The private pain of things so heavy that, some days, they're almost impossible to bear. Sickness. Grief. Depression. Anger. Bitterness. Doubt. Fear. Worry. Loneliness. They weigh us down, and sometimes, seem to suck the very life out of us. But be encouraged today. There is no earthly burden so heavy that God cannot or will not bear it for you. He is more than willing and able. Just ask Him!

Take Him With You:

There is no burden that God
cannot or will not bear for you.

All My Love, Jesus

Three Pebbles

For the Spirit God gave us does not make us timid,
but gives us power, love and self-discipline.
- II Timothy 1:7

Worry, doubt, and fear are three pebbles in the shoe of every believer. We sometimes live our lives with little or no true peace because of them. They are Satan's "What Ifs?" But God does not give us a spirit of fear, but He gives us a spirit of power, love, and a sound mind. A sound mind is always at peace, fully resting in and trusting God in every situation and circumstance we encounter. I'd rather have that than a pebble in my shoe any day!

Take Him With You:

A sound mind is always at peace.

Ron Lambros

God Wants It All

Then he said to them all:
"Whoever wants to be my disciple must deny themselves
and take up their cross daily and follow me."
- Luke 9:23

Why is it that so many believers demand 100% from God but give Him only a small percentage of ourselves? We want all of God's blessings, wisdom, guidance, and problem-solving abilities, and yet, we give Him only what we want to give Him, but not all of what we should. We hold back the anger, worry, grief, depression, fear, and doubt—and worse, the praise, honor, and thanksgiving He's due.

God wants it all! If you give Him 100%, you'll receive even more. I'll take that deal any day!

Take Him With You:

If you give God 100% of yourself,
you'll receive even more.

Leaving It to God

Commit your way to the Lord;
trust in him and he will do this...
- Psalm 37:5

All too often, we pray to God about a matter and then are either surprised that He actually answered it, or worse, we become resentful toward Him because He didn't answer it how or when we wanted Him to. We must realize that's not praying with believing faith! Praying is our part. Answering that prayer to our greatest benefit is God's part. God is faithful to answer our prayers, but we must always leave the how and when to Him!

Take Him With You:

Praying is your part. Answering it is God's.

Ron Lambros

Peaks and Valleys

He tends his flock like a shepherd: he gathers the lambs in his arms and carries them close to his heart...
- Isaiah 40:11

Valley days don't last forever, and neither do days on the mountaintop. In the roller coaster ride of life, we can go from the high days of joy and happiness to the low days of despair and depression. Nothing ever remains the same...except the Shepherd who leads us. God is always with us in every peak and valley of life, lifting us up from the lows and rejoicing with us in the highs. Trust Him to walk with you right where you are today.

Take Him With You:

God is with you in every peak and valley of your life.

You Get What You Choose

Do not be deceived: God cannot be mocked. A man reaps what he sows. Whoever sows to please their flesh will reap destruction; whoever sows to please the Spirit, from the Spirit will reap eternal life.
- Galatians 6:7, 8

Choices. We make thousands of them every day. In fact, our life is the sum total of the choices we've made, both good and bad, right and wrong.

Remember, you may not always get what you want, but you will always get what you choose! So base each choice on godly principles and precepts, and let the plumb-bob of each choice you make be based on God and His Word.

Choose wisely. It can be life-changing!

Take Him With You:
You may not get what you want, but you do get what you choose.

Groans

In the same way, the Spirit helps us in our weakness. We do not know what we ought to pray for, but the Spirit himself intercedes for us through wordless groans.
- Romans 8:25

There are times in the life of every believer when the pain is so great, the grief is so deep, the need is so far above us, that we are simply speechless in prayer. We cannot utter a single word. We can't fully verbalize all that our needy, breaking hearts wants to say.

All we can do is groan.

And God understands.

Be encouraged and rest assured that He hears and understands your words *and* your groans, He knows what your aching heart wants to verbalize and answers them both.

Take Him With You:

God hears and understands your groans.

God Understands

Jesus replied, "Foxes have dens and birds have nests,
but the Son of Man has no place to lay his head."
- Luke 9:58

We serve a Savior who understands our every trial and circumstance. He knows what it's like to be cold, lonely, hungry, betrayed, abandoned, mistreated, and misunderstood. He's stood at the grave of one He dearly loved and wept real tears. He was accused and wrongly convicted for something He did not do and paid the ultimate price for the very ones who accused Him.

Today, whatever you're facing, remember that He's already been right where you are, He understands, and will walk you through it.

Take Him With You:

God understands exactly what you're going through.

Ron Lambros

God's Silence

Wait for the Lord;
be strong and take heart and wait for the Lord.
- Psalm 27:14

God's silence can be deafening.

Those moments when we plead with Him in prayer, yet they seem to rise no higher than the ceiling, crashing broken and unanswered on the floor.

Always remember that God's silence does not mean His separation, for in that silence, God is often at work behind the scenes, working out the details to answer our prayers in the best way imaginable.

Trust Him in His silence. The answers will come.

Take Him With You:

God's silence does not mean His separation.

A Miracle-Working God

Now to him who is able to do immeasurably more
than all we ask or imagine...
- Ephesians 3:20

If we're really honest, many of us feel we sometimes have situations in our life that even God can't solve. They seem impossible to us. But the God who scooped out the Grand Canyon with His pinkie, breathed life into dust and created Man, spoke the universe into existence with but a word, and made a hummingbird's wings flutter just fast enough to allow it to hover, is still a miracle-working God. He can do exceedingly abundantly above all we can ask or even think!

Take Him With You:

God is still a miracle-working God!

Ron Lambros

God's Plan

In their hearts humans plan their course,
but the Lord establishes their steps.
- Proverbs 16:9

God's Word tells us that He has a plan for our lives—a plan to prosper us and not harm us, to give us hope and a future. Many times, life throws us a curve ball: the cancer is found, the spouse abandons, the job is lost, the prodigal leaves. By faith, we must accept each trial as part of His plan, and if we do, we know that He'll walk with us each step of the way and that all will work for our good if we only love and trust Him.

Take Him With You:

Accept your trials as part of God's plan for your life.

Trust Him for Today

But blessed is the one who trusts in the Lord, whose confidence is in him. They will be like a tree planted by the water that sends out its roots by the stream. It does not fear when heat comes; its leaves are always green. It has no worries in a year of drought and never fails to bear fruit.
- Jeremiah 17:7, 8

I have a confession to make: even as a minister, I sometimes struggle with my faith. Oh, I know that my eternal life is secure, that God loves me and will never leave me, and that He has never failed me—but it's in the day-to-day belief that I sometimes have difficulty. Simply put, I struggle with believing that God will always take care of me in each and every circumstance I face. I know that He can, but will He?

So I've purposed here and now to forget about yesterday and not worry about tomorrow. I will simply pray, "I will trust you for today!" and nothing more. If I stick with that, I know I can handle anything that life may throw at me, and that God will always be my sufficiency.

Take Him With You:

**Forget about yesterday and tomorrow,
and trust God for today.**

God's Design

God saw all that he had made, and it was very good.
- Genesis 1:31

Many times, we struggle with our significance. Does my life really matter, and what would really change if I were no longer here?

We all need to realize that long before there was a single drop of water in any ocean, before any star hung in the heavens, or before the first breath of wind blew across the landscape of time, God was there, and He designed you to be exactly who you are today.

Use the gifts and talents He's entrusted into your care wisely. You matter and count in His work!

Take Him With You:

God designed you to be exactly who you are.

Who Is Jesus?

"But what about you?" he asked. "Who do you say I am?"
- Matthew 16:15

In Matthew 16, Jesus asked the disciples a life-changing question: "*Who do you say that I am?*" He still asks each of us that very same question every day. And the way we answer it will reflect our spiritual depth and maturity, and ultimately, our eternal life.

Each of us must determine in our hearts who Jesus really is to us and what we will do with Him in our daily lives...how we will live, how we will relate to others, how we will trust, and how we will die.

The question is simple, but the answer can be life-changing and eternal!

Take Him With You:

Determine in your heart who Jesus really is to you.

Ron Lambros

Don't Give Up!

You need to persevere so that when you have done the will of God, you will receive what he has promised.
- Hebrews 10:36

Life isn't always fair. Many times, even with our best efforts, we fail and fall short of our dreams and our goals. But always remember that failure is never final, and it's in the perseverance and endurance that we are strengthened, we grow, and we mature in our faith.

If life has dealt you a difficult blow, don't give up! The God who created you enabled you to draw on His strength in your times of weakness, and through that, you will succeed!

Take Him With You:

For true success, draw on God's strength in your times of weakness.

God's Power of One

For just as through the disobedience of the one man the many were made sinners, so also through the obedience of the one man the many will be made righteous.
- Romans 5:19

God's Power of One: One angelic announcement. One virgin birth. One public ministry. One teacher and preacher. One triumphant entrance. One evening in the garden. One kiss. One betrayal. One mock trial. One savage beating. One crucifixion. One death. One tomb. One glorious resurrection from the dead. All for God to proclaim there is only One Way, One Truth, and One life for salvation!

And He did it all for One...you!

Take Him With You:

God sent Jesus into the world for you!

Wisdom

So give your servant a discerning heart to govern your people and to distinguish between right and wrong. For who is able to govern this great people of yours?
- I Kings 3:9

In I Kings, God asked Solomon, David's son and successor as King of Israel, what was the one thing that He could provide to him that Solomon desired most? Without hesitating, without blinking an eye, Solomon asked for wisdom and nothing more. And because of this, God blessed not only Solomon, but the people as well.

Maybe if our government leaders prayed and asked for wisdom every day, we all might be blessed, too!

Take Him With You:

**Ask God for wisdom for yourself
and for those in authority.**

True Contentment

I am not saying this because I am in need, for I have learned to be content whatever the circumstances.
- Philippians 4:11

Being content can be challenging. Our culture drives home our need for bigger and better, while God whispers, "I am all you need and I will give you all that you need. Trust me with your life."

What does it take to be truly content? Simply trusting that God made you just the way you are, that He wants the very best for you, that He has a plan and purpose for your life, and that He will provide all you need to get you there. It's not the world's definition of contentment—it's God's—and that's good enough for me!

Take Him With You:

Trusting God completely will bring you true contentment.

Ron Lambros

Let Down Your Nets

When he had finished speaking, he said to Simon, "Put out into deep water, and let down the nets for a catch." Simon answered, "Master, we've worked hard all night and haven't caught anything. But because you say so, I will let down the nets."
- Luke 5:4, 5

Are your nets wet?

Like Peter, we often try to do things on our own with no success. Then God shows up and tells us to try one more time, but this time, with His help and guidance. We argue, but finally give in...and that's when the answer comes!

Have you prayed for a loved one, a broken marriage, a wayward child, a financial miracle, a difficult circumstance—all with seemingly no results? Trust God, let down your nets just one more time, and see what He can do!

Take Him With You:

Your answer will come when you leave it in God's hands.

Dream Big!

Take delight in the Lord,
and he will give you the desires of your heart.
- Psalm 37:4

God has a plan and purpose for each of us, and deep within our hearts, He has added a very special place for our personal hopes and dreams. All too often, we allow life to stifle those dreams and squash our hopes.

But life has no mountain that God cannot level, no chasm that God cannot span. Whatever your dream is today, commit it to God, use it for His glory, and watch how your every hope and dream can become a reality.

And when you dream, dream big!

Take Him With You:

Commit all your hopes and dreams to God.

Being Accountable

So then, each of us will give an account of ourselves to God.
- Romans 14:12

Accountability. It's a critical part of life. First, we are accountable to God. He is our source of perfection, guidance, and example. Then, we are accountable to those around us: our spouse, family, friends, co-workers, employers. But we must never forget that we are also accountable to ourselves. We must constantly guard our health, heart, mind, and spirit, and always measure our spiritual stature at every moment of every day. Jesus set the bar that we must follow and seek to attain. To fall short of that goal is to live a life that will never reach its full potential.

Take Him With You:

You are accountable to God, to others, and to yourself.

God's Faithfulness

Know therefore that the Lord your God is God; he is the faithful God, keeping his covenant of love to a thousand generations of those who love him...
- Deuteronomy 7:9

The faithfulness of God is not based on how you feel, how you see things, or how good or bad the circumstances are around you at any given moment. The faithfulness of God is born in the heart of God Himself and is based solely on the purest and deepest love no mortal man can possibly comprehend. It is uncompromising, it is eternal, and it is everlasting. His love and faithfulness never fail or falter. With that, any day, any circumstance, or any situation can be faced with hope and confidence.

Know that God Himself is always working on your behalf!

Take Him With You:
You can always rest in the faithfulness of God.

True Faith

Now faith is confidence in what we hope for
and assurance about what we do not see.
- Hebrews 11:1

Faith is saying yes to whatever God wants you to do, even before you know what that is.

Take Him With You:

True faith is revealed when you trust God completely.

Wasted Energy

Who of you by worrying can add a single hour to your life?
- Luke 12:25

God must have a great deal of patience with us. How many times have we worried, fretted, or lost sleep over a situation; then, when we finally gave up trying to handle it in our own strength, God steps in, solves the problem, and then asks why we worried about it in the first place?

All too often, we have to come to the end of ourselves before God will do anything! Why waste the energy? Give Him your cares, concerns, and burdens, and let Him carry the load for you. He loves to do it, and it sure makes life easier and the journey more enjoyable!

Take Him With You:

Give God your cares, concerns, and burdens!

Denial

Jesus answered, "I tell you, Peter, before the rooster crows today, you will deny three times that you know me."
- Luke 22:34

Whether we admit it or not, like Peter, we've all had times when we've denied knowing Jesus Christ. We do it every day. We do it when:

- we're prompted by the Holy Spirit to share the Lord with someone and don't;
- we have an opportunity to help a person in need and don't;
- we turn the other way when someone "different" approaches us; or
- we do wrong rather than right because it's easier, more convenient, or the popular thing to do.

Actions like these break the heart of God! But, like Peter, you, too, can find forgiveness and the ability to be used by God once again.

Listen quietly in the recesses of your heart, and you might just hear the rooster crowing a third time!

Take Him With You:

Always be conscious of your actions.
They speak far louder than your words.

He's Praying for You

Christ Jesus who died—more than that,
who was raised to life—
is at the right hand of God and is also interceding for us.
- Romans 8:34

When facing difficult circumstances in life, knowing that someone is praying for us is always comforting. And the greatest blessing of all is knowing that the Scriptures assure us that Jesus Christ Himself is seated at the right hand of God the Father, making intercession for us every moment of every day.

Knowing the Lord Himself is praying for me personally gives me the confidence I need to face any situation or circumstance in my life and be victorious!

Take Him With You:

The Lord Himself is personally praying
for you at this very moment.

Ron Lambros

A Good Name

A good name is more desirable than great riches;
to be esteemed is better than silver or gold.
- Proverbs 22:1

Proverbs tells us that "*a good name is more desirable than great riches; to be esteemed is better than silver or gold.*" What do people think of when they hear your name mentioned? Does your name reflect honor, respect, and good character, or is it questionable?

Do absolutely everything you can to protect your name and your reputation. Have a name that not only honors God, but also carries on your godly legacy for generations to come.

Take Him With You:

Honor God by doing all you can to protect your name and your reputation.

Seeing Beyond the Façade

Anxiety weighs down the heart, but a kind word cheers it up.
- Proverbs 12:25

God allows us to come in contact with people every day who wear the smiles of success, happiness, and contentment, while deep within the recesses of their hearts, there is private pain and personal struggle. We must be sensitive to engage these individuals with compassion and encouragement.

Pray daily for the discernment necessary to see beyond their façade and do everything possible to help each one overcome the crushing pain they so easily hide.

Take Him With You:

Be sensitive to the hidden pain
and struggles of those around you.

Ron Lambros

Our Worth

For you know that it was not with perishable things
such as silver or gold that you were redeemed...
but with the precious blood of Christ...
- I Peter 1:18, 19

Too many people allow the world to define who they are. We are judged by the size of our homes, the cars we drive, the clothes we wear, our bank accounts, our social standing, and a host of other material standards which are subject to change at any given moment.

But our worth to God rests solely on our relationship with Him and His standard. The world sees the material worth of a person, but God judges our value to Him based on His unconditional love for us and by all that it cost Him to prove that love!

Take Him With You:

God values you more than you can possibly imagine.

The Blessings of God

I know that you can do all things;
no purpose of yours can be thwarted.
- Job 42:2

The blessings of God are not limited by time, space, or circumstance, but only by a heart that is cluttered with the cares, doubts, and fears this world often brings. Never think that God, or His ability to work in your life or in any situation, can be thwarted by anything, even your lack of faith. A sovereign God will work out His plan and purpose as He wills and sees fit to do...with or without you or your permission!

Take Him With You:

You cannot stop the perfect plan
and purpose of Almighty God.

Ron Lambros

Fulfill Your Dreams

Now may the God of peace...equip you with everything good for doing his will, and may he work in us what is pleasing to him, through Jesus Christ...
- Hebrews 13:20, 21

Many of us just go through the motions of everyday life. We're stuck in the rut of mediocrity, while our real dreams get put on the shelf. Life is far too short to waste doing the "good" instead of the "best." It's God's desire to fulfill your dreams every day.

Launch out in faith, break free, and pursue those dreams. God's will for your life is often revealed only after you take the first step.

So, what are you waiting for?

Take Him With You:

Take the first step toward your dreams.
God will help you get there.

God's Peace

Let the peace of Christ rule in your hearts...
- Colossians 3:15

We all face storms in our lives. We're prepared for some, while others take us completely by surprise, often with life-changing, faith-shaking results. Always remember that when Jesus calmed the storm on the Sea of Galilee with the simple phrase, *"Peace, be still!"*, He was also speaking to the hearts of each disciple in the boat. In every storm of life, He calms both the tempest and the fearful heart when we simply trust Him and yield to His sovereignty!

Take Him With You:

**God will give you perfect peace,
even in the greatest storms of your life.**

Ron Lambros

God's Eraser

If we confess our sins, he is faithful and just and will forgive us our sins and purify us from all unrighteousness.
- I John 1:9

God has a big eraser!

As we live each day, we often fail, make mistakes, and sin. We're human, with a will of our own, and we just can't help it! Isn't it comforting to know that God is ready to not only forgive our sin, but to also erase it completely for all eternity when we approach Him with a broken and repentant heart?

Take your biggest sin to God. His eraser is always guided by mercy, forgiveness, and unconditional love.

Take Him With You:

God can forgive your biggest sin.

God's Palette

For it is God who works in you to will and to act
in order to fulfill his good purpose.
- Philippians 2:13

Unconditional love is found on God's paint palette, each color brushed on by the Master's hand with gentle strokes of understanding and forgiveness. That hidden sin? Covered with His first coat. That blunder or mistake? Second stroke, gladly applied. That habitual sin or moral failure? Another coat brushed on with His loving hand. God's palette never runs dry. And with each coat, God creates His masterpiece of perfection in you.

Take Him With You:

God will cover your greatest sin with His paintbrush of unconditional love.

Be Passionate!

For where your treasure is, there your heart will be also.
- Matthew 6:21

A network rep just left my office. He made a tremendous presentation, but he lacked the one thing I wanted to see: a passion for, and belief in, that which he presented. He didn't make the sale. After all, if he doesn't have a passion and belief in what he's selling, why should I?

Maybe that's why so many are ineffective as they share Jesus Christ. People always need to see passion and belief in what we're sharing!

Take Him With You:

Your passion for Jesus Christ
often speaks louder than your words.

You Matter to God

...but God has surely listened and has heard my prayer.
- Psalm 66:19

One of the most incredible things about God is the fact that when I pray, He quiets all the noise of heaven and earth, stops absolutely everything He's doing, bends His ear in my direction, and listens intently to all that I'm saying to Him.

The very thought of the God of the universe quieting the angels and the din of all He's created just to hear my heartfelt cries lets me know that He loves me, He cares about me, and that I matter to Him!

Take Him With You:

You always have God's full attention when you pray.

Ron Lambros

The World of Want

The Lord is my shepherd, I lack nothing.
- Psalm 23:1

So many people today lie trapped in the "world of want." They all want more than they have and feel that their happiness lies in the bigger paycheck, the larger home, the special vacation, the promotion, the marriage to that certain someone, or a host of other wants their hearts desire. But all we should truly want lies in God Himself, for, "*The Lord is my Shepherd; I shall not want.*" He'll always give you all you ever really need.

Take Him With You:

God will always give you everything you really need.

A God of Second Chances

"Come now, let us settle the matter," says the Lord. "Though your sins are like scarlet, they shall be as white as snow; though they are red as crimson, they shall be like wool."
- Isaiah 1:18

Our God is a God of second chances.

Isn't that comforting?

All of us know someone who could use a second chance today—maybe even you personally. The siren song of sin and temptation is often too much for us to withstand, or the pressures of life cause us to cave in. When that happens, God invites us to come to Him, and though our "*sins are like scarlet, they will be white as snow.*"

Second chances are always a blessing to receive and give.

Take Him With You:

Our God is a God of second chances.

The Measure of Your Heart

My son, give me your heart
and let your eyes delight in my ways.
- Proverbs 23:26

Fame and wealth may earn the world's accolades, but they don't impress God. He seeks those who possess a humble spirit, living a life of obedience and sacrifice.

When God takes the measure of a person, He places the tape measure around the heart and not the head. The size of our heart and all it contains not only impresses God, but also brings Him the greatest joy.

May each heart be found pleasing to its Creator.

Take Him With You:

God always measures the size and content of your heart.

Icing on the Cupcake

Every good and perfect gift is from above,
coming down from the Father of the heavenly lights,
who does not change like shifting shadows.
- James 1:17

Many believers go through life with the mistaken idea that God will bless us and answer our prayers just because we are His children and we ask Him to do it. The reality we must accept is that God is a God of love and infinite wisdom, and He answers all of our prayers according to His good and perfect will for our lives.

The other reality we must embrace is that, after salvation, God owes us absolutely nothing! He has given us *everything* at Calvary. Everything after that is simply icing on the cupcake!

Take Him With You:

God gave you everything at Calvary.

Ron Lambros

Unforgiveness

For if you forgive other people when they sin against you, your heavenly Father will also forgive you. But if you do not forgive others their sins, your Father will not forgive your sins.
- Matthew 6:14, 15

Many of our hearts are jailed by unforgiveness. We harbor anger and bitterness towards someone, and it soon becomes the heavy weight we carry with us everywhere. We wake up with it every morning and go to bed with it every night.

Whether you believe your feelings are justified or not, unforgiveness has no place in the heart of any believer because God will not forgive us until we first forgive. God will open the cell bars that imprison our hearts only after we first provide Him with the key of our own forgiveness towards others.

Take Him With You:

Unforgiveness has no place in your heart.

God's Restoration

Create in me a pure heart, O God, and renew a steadfast spirit within me. Do not cast me from your presence or take your Holy Spirit from me. Restore to me the joy of your salvation and grant me a willing spirit, to sustain me.
- Psalm 51:10-12

At one time or another, every believer goes through a time when our spirits are weak, tired, and spent. Sometimes, we even feel hopeless.

We need to encourage ourselves that even King David, who the Bible refers to as *"a man after God's own heart,"* possessed a weary and broken spirit. Sin had taken its toll, and he cried out to God for restoration. David received his renewal because God restores the heart and soul that humbly seek Him.

Take Him With You:

God will restore your heart if you humbly seek Him.

Acting on Your Own

Those who live according to the flesh have their minds set on what the flesh desires; but those who live in accordance with the Spirit have their minds set on what the Spirit desires.
- Romans 8:5

Sometimes, we become so strongly attracted to—or passionate about—a given something or someone, that we act on our own without any regard for God's permission or leading.

When confronted with the temptation to do so, wait until you have the power and guidance of the Holy Spirit. Passion without God's purpose, permission, or presence can become unbridled worldliness, no matter the best of intentions.

Seek God first!

Take Him With You:

Seek God first in everything you do.

Knocking Off the Cobwebs

Dear friends, do not be surprised at the fiery ordeal that has come on you to test you, as though something strange were happening to you. But rejoice inasmuch as you participate in the sufferings of Christ, so that you may be overjoyed when his glory is revealed.
- I Peter 4:12, 13

God does not want our faith kept in mothballs, so He sometimes allows trials and testing to come into our lives; the unexpected hardships and heartbreaks that rock us in places we never thought we'd face as a child of God. And it's in those defining moments that we knock off the cobwebs of our everyday faith and face life with a new and improved one that's empowered by God Himself.

That's a gift we should embrace and desire!

Take Him With You:

Your faith will always grow stronger through trials if you let it.

Ron Lambros

Everyday Faith

I have been crucified with Christ and I no longer live, but Christ lives in me. The life I now live in the body, I live by faith in the Son of God, who loved me and gave himself for me.
- Galatians 2:20

Faith is exhibited when circumstances are dire and the need for it is great. But true faith is revealed more in the humdrum drudgery of life.

God wants us to hold fast to our faith when we need it the most—yes—but He wants us to show it even more in the details of our everyday lives: the common, everyday events we all face and live out. Consistent, day-by-day faith speaks volumes to the hearts of those who are watching us.

Take Him With You:

Your true faith shows every day.

God Never Changes

I the Lord do not change.
- Malachi 3:6

It's easy to praise God when the sun is shining, life is good, and your cares are easy. But it's another thing to praise God in the dark days, when life is hard, feelings are raw, and your doubts and fears throw your emotions into a blender and produce spiritual uncertainty.

God never changes!

Always remember that the same God who is with you in the good days is the same God who holds your hand and leads you through the dark days as well!

Take Him With You:

God is with you every moment of every day.

Ron Lambros

Defining Moments of Faith

Even though I walk through the darkest valley, I will fear no evil, for you are with me; your rod and your staff, they comfort me.
- Psalm 23:4

"*I thank God for the mountains, and I thank Him for the valleys, I thank Him for the storms He brought me through. For if I'd never had a problem, I wouldn't know God could solve them, I'd never know what faith in God could do.*" *- Andrae Crouch.*

No one enjoys valley days—times of testing and grief—but they are the defining moments of our faith and the times when God shows His sovereignty and unconditional love. Don't run from these moments, embrace them, trusting God through it all!

Take Him With You:

Trust God in your valley days.
They are the defining moments of your faith.

The Power of Prayer

The prayer of a righteous person is powerful and effective.
- James 5:16

We hear much today about our dependence on fossil fuels and other limited energy resources. But as a people and Nation, we often overlook our need for the most ignored, yet most available source of true power: the power of prayer. While a gallon of gas might get you to the market or work, prayer can bring healing, comfort, wisdom, guidance, and direction for daily living. And it is in prayer that you find the true power and presence of Almighty God!

Take Him With You:

You have unlimited power in prayer.

Getting Clean

I will cleanse them from all the sin they have committed against me and will forgive all their sins of rebellion against me.
- Jeremiah 33:8

We all struggle with sin. Even though we read our Bible, pray, faithfully attend church, and truly love God, in the daily grind of life, we often slip and wallow in the mire of ungodliness.

Always remember that if Jesus instructed Peter to repeatedly forgive someone who sins against him, how much more will a loving God forgive us when we earnestly repent, seeking cleansing and forgiveness?

His love is deep, wide, and unconditional!

Take Him With You:

God is ready and willing to forgive your every sin.

That Settles It!

Salvation is found in no one else, for there is no other name under heaven given to mankind by which we must be saved.
- Acts 4:12

Many believers sometimes doubt their salvation. It's the "If I were really saved, I wouldn't act this way, feel this way, or say or do these things" syndrome.

These doubts come along when we base our entire salvation experience on OUR feelings, OUR actions, and OUR words. But the reality is that our salvation is secured by believing what Jesus Christ did on the cross for each of us—nothing more and nothing less—and that settles it! Period!

Take Him With You:
Your salvation is based on Jesus Christ and His sacrifice, and nothing else.

Ron Lambros

God's Loving Pursuit

My sacrifice, O God, is a broken spirit;
a broken and contrite heart you, God, will not despise.
- Psalm 51:17

Ever feel like you've crossed the line once too often with God? That this time you've really gone too far and sinned one time too many?

Always remember that the shepherd left the 99 in the flock to find the one that strayed, the peasant woman went to great lengths to find the one coin that fell from the ten, and the father patiently waited for the prodigal of his two sons to return.

You can never escape God's loving pursuit or His forgiveness when you seek Him with a broken and repentant heart!

Take Him With You:

You can never outrun the loving pursuit of God.

Enough for Today

Give us today our daily bread.
- Matthew 6:11

With each new morning, we should pray and ask God for the wisdom, strength, and power we'll need for that day's challenges. And God answers with His infinite wisdom, "*I'll give you enough for today.*" Like the manna and quail received each day during the Exodus, God does not promise us anything for tomorrow. Instead, He promises He'll give us all we'll need for that day and that day alone. And what He gives is always enough!

Take Him With You:

God gives you everything you need for today.

Providing for His Plan

The Lord works out everything to its proper end...
- Proverbs 16:4

God always provides whatever is necessary to bring His plans and purpose to pass. He made the tree from which the cross would come, the iron from which the nails would be made, the thorny vine that would be fashioned into a torturous crown, and placed Jesus and Judas within their mother's wombs. All were part of His plan for our salvation. And He has a plan and purpose for our lives as well, and has provided, or will provide, absolutely everything that is needed to bring it to pass.

Take Him With You:

God will provide everything that's needed
for His plan and purpose to happen.

More than Conquerors!

...we are more than conquerors through him who loved us.
- Romans 8:37

Battle lines are drawn in the sand of our lives every day. Satan hurls his weapons of fear, doubt, worry, illness, depression, loneliness, and everything else he can think of to rob us of the joy and abundant life we possess in Jesus Christ.

Yet on our side stands a humble General, slipping quietly into the fray through a lowly manger and winning each battle with the weapon of a Roman cross.

And in Him alone, we are more than conquerors because He loves us.

Take Him With You:

You are more than a conqueror through Jesus Christ.

Ron Lambros

The Love of God

This is love: not that we loved God, but that he loved us and sent his Son as an atoning sacrifice for our sins.
- I John 4:10

What mortal, human mind can truly comprehend the love of God? Who can possibly understand its depths and enormity? Who can fathom its measure and unconditional nature?

Never in the heart of man can His love be fully grasped, but it can be received!

We do not have to understand the hows and whys of God's love. We have but to take it by faith and accept the greatest gift imaginable: salvation through His Son, Jesus Christ!

Take Him With You:

God's love for you cannot be fully grasped or measured, but it can be received.

A Little More

Lord, you alone are my portion and my cup;
you make my lot secure.
- Psalm 16:5

Today's culture teaches us the concept of "a little more." For true joy, happiness, and contentment, we need "a little more" money, house, car, boat, stocks, and bonds. More *stuff!*

But God's method is far simpler. He tells us that one cross, one thorny crown, three rusty nails, and one loving Savior who takes away our sin is truly all we need...nothing more...it is enough, and it is finished!

We should never want or need anything more.

Take Him With You:

You don't need anything more than Jesus!

Ron Lambros

All Things Are Possible!

I keep my eyes always on the Lord. With him at my right hand, I will not be shaken. Therefore my heart is glad and my tongue rejoices; my body also will rest secure...
- Psalm 16:8, 9

Someone once said that a person can live without food for 40 days, without water for 3 days, and without air for 8 minutes, but a person cannot live one second without hope.

Many times in our lives, we lose hope. Despite all of our prayers and all of our pleadings, our situations or circumstances seem impossible to us.

But remember, our weakest moments allow God to show Himself to be His strongest, and with God, all things are possible!

Take Him With You:

Never forget, with God, all things are possible!

God's Perfect Plan

For this God is our God for ever and ever;
he will be our guide even to the end.
- Psalm 48:14

Many people believe that their lives are controlled by fate. They believe that their own hard work, sheer luck, good fortune, or just plain chance determines their success or failure in life.

But for a child of God, the future is clear. God has a perfect, specific plan for each of us, and while we may not always understand our circumstances, we can be assured that our lives are always lovingly guided by His purpose, presence, and permission.

Take Him With You:

God has a perfect plan for your life.

Ron Lambros

Your Greatest Worth

For Christ also suffered once for sins,
the righteous for the unrighteous, to bring you to God.
- I Peter 3:18

Many people derive their worth and self-esteem through their position in their home, workplace, church, or community. They seek the status, accolades, and recognition of man to feel their value.

But God has placed incredible worth on each of us simply because we are His creation and design. And He proved it when He sent Jesus Christ to die on the cross for YOU, even if you were the only person on the face of the earth.

You won't find greater worth or value than that!

Take Him With You:

Don't sell yourself short.
You have incredible value to God.

You Are Not God!

But I the Lord will speak what I will, and it shall be fulfilled without delay. For in your days, you rebellious people, I will fulfill whatever I say, declares the Sovereign Lord.
- Ezekiel 12:25

The reason many believers (and churches) today do not see God work miracles, or do not have the blessings that He intends for them, is that they tend to compartmentalize Him, putting Him in a box. They feel they know how God thinks, how He will act, or what He will do in any given situation.

THAT'S NOT GOD!

The all-knowing and all-powerful God still works miracles today when we acknowledge that He is God...and we are not.

Take Him With You:

**You can see God's miracles
if you look for them with a humble heart.**

Ron Lambros

Focus on the Cross

*...let us throw off everything that hinders and the sin
that so easily entangles. And let us run with perseverance
the race marked out for us, fixing our eyes on Jesus,
the pioneer and perfecter of faith.*
- Hebrews 12:1, 2

It's easy to lose focus.

Distractions and circumstances often cause us to settle for simply doing *good* things instead of doing *great* things. Too often, we focus on our careers, personal desires, and goals at the expense of our families and our spiritual growth.

To truly keep life in balance, always focus on the Cross of Christ. Your life's perspective will always be eternally-minded, and your life will be lived to its fullest potential.

Take Him With You:

**To keep your life in balance,
always focus on the Cross of Christ.**

He Drew the Map

Let the morning bring me word of your unfailing love,
for I have put my trust in you. Show me the way I should go,
for to you I entrust my life.
- Psalm 143:8

There are days when we awake to find ourselves in spiritually uncharted waters, days when the challenges and circumstances of life place before us obstacles we have never faced before.

It's encouraging to know that our Heavenly Father drew the map and plotted the course we would be on at any given moment in our life and, if we ask, He will give us all we need to reach the destination He has chosen for each of us.

Take Him With You:

God will give you all you need
to bring His plan for your life to pass.

Ron Lambros

You Are Everything

See what great love the Father has lavished on us, that we should be called children of God! And that is what we are!
- I John 3:1

Some days, it's easy to feel small and insignificant, struggling to find meaning and purpose in life. But always remember that God created you for greatness! He has numbered the hairs on your head and the years of your life. He has written your name in the palm of His hand and calls you by name. He has even called you His child and Heir of His Kingdom.

Never feel worthless or insignificant. To God, you are everything!

Take Him With You:

God created you for greatness,
and, to Him, you are everything.

Your Legacy

I have no greater joy than to hear
that my children are walking in the truth.
- III John 4

Too many people blame their heritage and upbringing for their ungodly behavior and troubled life-style today. While it may be true that we cannot control much about our past, with God's help, we do have the ability to control our future and the legacy that we can leave behind. There is more to this life than leaving a great inheritance and simple memories. Each of us should leave behind a great legacy.

May we be found faithful to make it a rich and godly one for the generations that follow!

Take Him With You:

Begin right now and purpose in your heart
to leave a godly legacy.

Beauty for Ashes

...to bestow on them a crown of beauty instead of ashes, the oil of joy instead of mourning, and a garment of praise instead of a spirit of despair. They will be called oaks of righteousness, a planting of the Lord for the display of his splendor.
- Isaiah 61:3

Life's trials and circumstances are sometimes easy for us to handle. But other times, they envelope our lives like a raging wildfire, consuming everything in its path—our emotions, strength, dreams, hopes, and sometimes, even our faith.

But our God is a God of restoration, and He alone can take the ashes of ruin from a life spent and withered by each firestorm and craft them into an object of His beauty and grace.

Take Him With You:

God alone can turn the ashes of your life into something beautiful.

Believe God Will

If you believe, you will receive whatever you ask for in prayer.
- Matthew 21:22

There are days in every believer's life when our faith will be tested. No one is immune. Even those with years of seeing God's handiwork in their lives are often sorely tested, almost to the breaking point.

It is in those divinely intimate moments that we realize it takes far more faith to believe God *will* than to believe God *can*. God can do anything, but we must hold resolutely to our belief that He will do it!

Take Him With You:

True faith is when you know God can,
but believe God will.

Ron Lambros

Come and Rest

*That is why, for Christ's sake, I delight in weaknesses,
in insults, in hardships, in persecutions, in difficulties.
For when I am weak, then I am strong.
- II Corinthians 12:10*

There are moments in life that knock our feet out from under us. They come with no warning and suck the very life out of us, leaving us bruised, battered, bewildered, and numb. We confidently quote Scripture and lean on our faith, but even this, sometimes, just doesn't seem enough to overcome the tempest.

But once your heart is empty...that's when God invites us to come and find rest in Him. And it's only there that our comfort and answers are truly found.

Take Him With You:

**You can find true rest and strength
when you accept God's invitation to "come."**

Walking with God

The Lord makes firm the steps of the one who delights in him...
- Psalm 37:23

God desires to walk with us daily, leading our lives as He's planned. But all too often, we get tired of just walking at His pace, and we run ahead on our own, thinking that we know the path and the plan better than He does.

And without fail, we stumble and fall, and return to Him bruised and battered because of our ignorance and impatience.

Remember, walking with God always leads you to the right place at the right time for the right reason.

Take Him With You:

Your life's journey will always work out best
if you let God do the leading.

Ron Lambros

He Will Make a Way

The Lord himself goes before you and will be with you;
he will never leave you nor forsake you.
Do not be afraid; do not be discouraged.
- Deuteronomy 31:8

Ever experience a "Red Sea moment?" Those times where the pressures and problems of life confront you head-on, all while your back is up against a seemingly impenetrable wall, with no way of escape or rescue in sight?

It's in these very moments that God loves to prove His incredible ability to miraculously clear a path for you, to help you overcome whatever challenge, difficulty, or obstacle you may be facing.

Cling to your faith today, no matter how small. He can and will make a way for you!

Take Him With You:

God will make a way for you if you only believe.

All My Love, Jesus

Safely Home

...you were bought at a price.
- I Corinthians 6:20

Have you ever noticed that when you purchase something of great value, you take extra good care of it? You carry it just a bit more cautiously, being careful not to bump or break it, and you secure it safely until you get it home?

God's Word tells us that we have each been "*bought with a price.*" Jesus sacrificed everything for us. And if He did that, we're valuable enough to God for Him to take extra good care of us each day...and to pull out all the stops to get us safely home!

Take Him With You:

God will do whatever it takes to get you safely home.

Ron Lambros

Our Humanity

Do you not know? Have you not heard? The Lord is the everlasting God, the Creator of the ends of the earth. He will not grow tired or weary, and his understanding no one can fathom.
- Isaiah 40:28

It's difficult to always understand God's ways.

Why He allows some things and not others.

Why He does things one way and not another.

Why He answers some prayers and pleadings and seems to ignore others.

In our humanity, we can't always understand the sovereignty of a holy and righteous God, but we can always trust Him. And we can know that no matter what He does or how He does it, His actions are always done with perfect love and always with our best interest at heart!

Take Him With You:

**You may not always understand God,
but you can always trust Him.**

Never Underestimate the Power of God!

And these are but the outer fringe of his works;
how faint the whisper we hear of him!
Who then can understand the thunder of his power?
- Job 26:14

As each new day comes, you might find yourself feeling frightened, worried, or afraid. The economy is bad, wars continue around the world, crime is rampant, and it seems like the world is out of control. Or perhaps you've lost your job with no prospects in sight, your marriage has failed and appears beyond repair, a wayward child has left you heart-broken, the disease is terminal, a loved one has died and left you all alone, or you wonder where the money is going to come from to pay the bills.

In these times—and every other situation or circumstance of life—NEVER UNDERESTIMATE THE POWER OF GOD! He always has your best interest at heart, He's in absolute control of each and every situation, He can turn even the bad into good, and He will move Heaven and earth to accomplish His plan and purpose for your life. You can trust Him in all things!

Take Him With You:

God is able to do things you can't imagine!
Never underestimate His power!

Ron Lambros

How Big is Your Faith?

He replied, "If you have faith as small as a mustard seed,
you can say to this mulberry tree, 'Be uprooted and planted
in the sea,' and it will obey you."
- Luke 17:6

A question we often hear is, "How big is God?"

God is big enough to solve any problem, big enough to forgive any sin, big enough to comfort the deepest grief, big enough to walk with you through any valley, big enough to help you realize your greatest dreams, and big enough to help you overcome any obstacle or fear in life.

The question is not, "How big is God?" The question is, "How big is your faith in Him?"

Take Him With You:

How big is your faith in God?
You'll find that He's big enough for anything!

God's Filter of Love

And we know that in all things God works for the good of those who love him, who have been called according to his purpose.
- Romans 8:28

Things often happen in life that we simply don't understand. The world says God is to blame, while the child of God knows that He lovingly allowed it. There is a difference! When God allows something to occur, it is always filtered by His unfathomable love, it is part of His perfect plan and purpose for our life, and we are promised that even the most tragic of events will work for our good if we simply trust and have an unwavering faith in Him.

Take Him With You:

If God allows something to happen, it has a valuable purpose for your life.

Ron Lambros

White as Snow

Wash me, and I shall be whiter than snow.
- Psalm 51:7

Looking out my window at the snow-covered landscape blanketing my neighborhood, I thought of the words of the Prophet Isaiah who penned, "*Though your sins be as scarlet, they shall be as white as snow.*"

Thanks to Jesus, our sins, our vilest and most offensive acts toward God, can be made as pure and clean as the snow that hangs from the branches of the trees outside.

That makes me thankful and glad.

Enjoy the snow!

Take Him With You:

You have committed no sin that Jesus' blood cannot forgive.

Trust Him with Today

"For I know the plans I have for you," declares the Lord,
"plans to prosper you and not harm you,
plans to give you hope and a future."
- Jeremiah 29:11

God says, "*I know what I'm doing. I have it all planned out—plans to take care of you, not abandon you, plans to give you the future you hope for.*" (Jeremiah 29:11. The Message).

When all of our plans fall through and our situation seems hopeless, that's when God does His greatest work as only He can do. Remember, if you can trust Him with your eternity, you can surely trust Him with today! Stay faithful!

Take Him With You:

If you can trust God for eternity,
you can trust Him with today.

Simple Worship

Therefore encourage one another and build each other up,
just as in fact you are doing.
- I Thessalonians 5:11

I worshiped a few moments ago at the bank. It wasn't much. I just encouraged someone who needed it. I've learned that a kind word shared with someone who needs it is worship. To those who are loved much, that kind word may be nothing more than a crumb. But to those starved for kindness, it can be a banquet!

Share a word of hope and encouragement with someone today. That's worship at its best!

Take Him With You:

Your simplest acts of kindness are worship.

Lessons in the Wait

Be still before the Lord and wait patiently for him.
- Psalm 37:7

Waiting on God is never easy until you realize that there's power and purpose in the wait! The answers to your prayers are not always God's highest priority. Many times, it's what He wants to teach you about Himself in the wait that proves to be the greatest blessing.

Pray for answers, yes, but pray, too, for God to teach you more about Himself in that wait. You'll find rich lessons learned in the process.

Take Him With You:

God has many lessons to teach you as you wait on Him.

Ron Lambros

What God Has Done for You

My mouth will tell of your righteous deeds, of your saving acts all day long—though I know not how to relate them all. I will come and proclaim your mighty acts, Sovereign Lord; I will proclaim your righteous deeds, yours alone. Since my youth, God, you have taught me, and to this day I declare your marvelous deeds. Even when I am old and gray, do not forsake me, my God, till I declare your power to the next generation, your mighty acts to all who are to come.
- Psalm 71:15-18

A woman called our ministry recently and wanted to know how to be born again. I shared numerous Scriptures with her, but she just could not comprehend or begin to grasp the concept of God's grace. I finally simply shared with her what Jesus Christ had done in my own personal life. That's all it took and she was gloriously saved.

People can argue and debate doctrine and theology, but no one can argue what God has done for you personally.

Now, go and share Jesus!

Take Him With You:

Sharing what Jesus has done in your life is the best evangelism.

Seeing Things Like God Does

Open my eyes that I may see wonderful things in your law.
- Psalm 119:18

Each day, we are faced with personal choices and circumstances in our life. And all too often, it's difficult to know exactly what to do.

When faced with such a situation, remember that trusting God is not seeing things as they appear to be to us, but rather seeing things as they appear to God. When filtered from that perspective, our answers will become clear, and God will bless as He gently leads and guides us.

Take Him With You:

Trusting God is reinforced
when you try to see things as He does.

Ron Lambros

Accept His Answer

For the word of the Lord is right and true;
he is faithful in all he does.
- Psalm 33:4

A tragedy we often face when praying is missing God's answer because He did it in a way that we weren't expecting.

How many times do we pray but look for Him to answer as we desire or expect Him to? That's not God! He always answers our prayers with wisdom and knowledge far above our own.

You pray, yes, but let Him answer as He wills to do, and accept His answer as your own! It will always work for your good!

Take Him With You:

God always answers our prayers
in ways that are best for us.

State of the Church

For I am not ashamed of the gospel, because it is the power
of God that brings salvation to everyone who believes...
- Romans 1:16

I just had a great conversation with a close friend about the "state of the church" in today's culture. It's difficult to fathom that the church has reached the low point that it has in so many ways. Far too many churches have compromised or traded the Gospel for cultural tolerance, political correctness, and high-tech performance.

That just means that people will bust hell wide-open with a watered-down message, awesome sound, and 3-D glasses!

Take Him With You:

The life-changing power of any church
is the Gospel of Jesus Christ!

Ron Lambros

Wireless Communication

But when you pray, go into your room, close the door and pray to your Father, who is unseen. Then your Father, who sees what is done in secret, will reward you.
- Matthew 6:6

I just sat through an incredibly informative teaching session on utilizing emerging technologies in worship, both corporately and individually. Social media, the internet, radio, television, video streaming, and satellite are all relevant and cutting edge.

While I sat there listening, it occurred to me that believers have always had the finest wireless communication available at any time. It's called prayer. We just need to use it more often.

Take Him With You:

Your greatest form of wireless communication is prayer.

Ordinary People

Moses said to the Lord, "Pardon your servant, Lord. I have never been eloquent, neither in the past nor since you have spoken to your servant. I am slow of speech and tongue."

The Lord said to him, "Who gave human beings their mouths? Who makes them deaf or mute? Who gives them sight or makes them blind? Is it not I, the Lord? Now go; I will help you speak and will teach you what to say."

- Exodus 4:10-12

Far too many people go through life with the mistaken idea that they are useless in God's grand scheme of things. But God used an illiterate shepherd to lead His people out of bondage, a young boy with a sling and five smooth stones to defeat a giant and become King of God's chosen people, and a small baby in a manger to become the ultimate King of Kings.

If life has taught us anything, it's that God can use the ordinary to accomplish the extraordinary...and that includes you!

Take Him With You:

God is more interested in your availability than your ability.

Ron Lambros

God Never Changes

God is not human, that he should lie, nor a human being, that he should change his mind. Does he not speak and then not act? Does he promise and not fulfill?
- Numbers 23:19

Every day won't always be pleasant, enjoyable, or filled with joy and happiness. Life can be cruel, and heartaches and painful days will come. But remember that God is always with you, in the good days and the bad, and that His silence never means His separation. The sun will still rise tomorrow, the skies will clear, and your perspective will change. Simply hold on to the fact that He is always God, He always loves you, and He never changes!

Take Him With You:

Remember that God is always with you
and He never changes.

God Can Mend the Broken

He heals the brokenhearted and binds up their wounds.
- Psalm 147:3

It's never easy when you find out that someone you trusted and considered a friend was actually a Judas, kissing your cheek while counting the 30 pieces of silver behind your back. In this life, some people will disappoint you and breach a sacred trust. But God can work the broken and most painful situations into the most blessed and beneficial for your life when your trust is in Him completely and alone.

Take Him With You:

**God can take life at its worst
and make it a blessing in your life.**

Ron Lambros

A Place of Worship

Enter his gates with thanksgiving and his courts with praise; give thanks to him and praise his name. For the Lord is good and his love endures forever; his faithfulness continues through all generations.
- Psalm 100:4, 5

The daily grind. Sometimes it makes us lose perspective. But we can quit dreading the Mondays of life when we make our work worship, our desk an altar, and our office a place of spiritual refuge and prayer.

Do you serve a corporation or a Kingdom? Do you live to work or make your work worship? Do you only want a paycheck or do you want to make a difference?

It's all about your perspective, your attitude, and who gets the glory and the praise.

Take Him With You:

Honor God today by making your work worship.

He Made You Priceless

Do not fear, for I have redeemed you;
I have summoned you by name; you are mine.
- Isaiah 43:1

What are you really worth? The world says you're nothing more than a paycheck, a commodity to be exchanged, traded for a less expensive replacement or sold to the highest bidder. But God's value of your life is far greater. He took a handful of dirt and breathed into it His very breath. Then, He measured your worth with one wooden cross, one crown of thorns and three rusty nails. And by doing that, He made you priceless.

Live like it!

Take Him With You:

You are priceless to God.

Ron Lambros

I Will Trust You

Though he slay me, yet will I hope in him.
- Job 13:15

Dear God-

Even when those I love or trust the most disappoint me and let me down, still I will trust you. Even when I walk in fear and uncertainty because of my circumstances, still I will trust you. Even when I hurt emotionally and have no desire to even breathe, still I will trust you. Even when the doctor says it isn't good news or my employer says I no longer matter, still I will trust you. Even when I don't think I can put one foot in front of the other and carry on, still I will trust you. Even when I'm filled with fear, doubt, worry, anxiety, regret, sorrow, or grief, still I will trust you.

I will trust you because I know that one day my life will be over and I will be free from all the pain and strife of daily living. And it is then—*especially then*—that I will trust you...not for the moment, not for the day, not just for the circumstance, but for eternity.

And that makes it all worthwhile.

Take Him With You:

**This life has no pain or sorrow
that your trust in God won't overcome.**

His Love

Dear friends, let us love one another,
for love comes from God. Everyone who loves has been
born of God and knows God. Whoever does not love does
not know God, because God is love.
- I John 4:7, 8

Betrayal. We've all felt its painful sting. Jesus felt it in the Garden with a gentle kiss surrounded by the sounds of clinking silver coins and soldier's feet. You may have felt it, too. The spouse who said, "I do," but didn't. The business partner who said, "we will," but did it on his own and left you high and dry. The child who promised he would honor and obey but disappointed and broke your heart. The friend you felt would always understand and support you but became the very one who spread the gossip, abandoned you in your time of need, or personally drove the dagger the deepest into your heart.

The world is full of betrayers, those who breach your trust, break your heart, and leave you bruised and battered on the floor of life like a dime-store mirror. But God is a God of truth, the only one who cannot lie and never disappoints. He is the one you can count on when you can't count on anyone else.

Sadly, we often rely on others more than we rely on Him, but He still waits patiently for us to realize He's always there and will always do what's best for us in every situation.

Accept His invitation for Him to prove His love to you. It's real, it's true, and it never fails!

Take Him With You:

**God is the only person you can always rely on
and trust completely!**

"Thomas" Moments

For we live by faith, not by sight.
- II Corinthians 5:7

Even the most seasoned believer can have a "Thomas" moment, a time when what you're asked to believe or to trust is so far beyond anything your mind or heart can comprehend that you say you will not believe it until you see it with your own eyes.

Don't rest in the physical confirmation of your faith, but rather believe in the supernatural workings of a loving, caring, and compassionate God who simply says, "Trust me."

Take Him With You:

When God says you can trust Him, you can with absolutely no doubt!

Ron Lambros

Vengeance

Do not take revenge, my dear friends,
but leave room for God's wrath, for it is written:
"It is mine to avenge; I will repay," says the Lord.
- Romans 12:19

If we're honest, we all face those moments when we want nothing more than to exact revenge on someone, to make them feel the same hurt and pain that they have inflicted on us or someone we love.

When we have these feelings, God's Word must control our hearts, and we must remember that He is a God who seeks and serves justice, and that vengeance is His alone to do when and how He sees fit...and He will in His time!

Take Him With You:

God is a God of justice.
Leave your desire for revenge to Him.

God Still Speaks

My sheep listen to my voice; I know them, and they follow me.
- John 10:27

Many of us want to hear God's voice, but we struggle. Too often, we expect to hear Him in the thundering of majestic words, when He often chooses to speak in a soft, gentle whisper.

But He does speak!

He speaks to us when we pray and when we read His Word. He also speaks through His Church and godly counsel. But He will only speak to a heart that has been prepared to receive all that He wants to share, one that is filled with brokenness, repentance, expectation, and thanksgiving.

Take Him With You:

Prepare your heart and God will speak to you today.

Ron Lambros

Surrender It!

I can do all this through him who gives me strength.
- Philippians 4:13

Many times in our lives, we come face-to-face with obstacles or circumstances that we simply can't control. No matter how hard we try, with all that's in us, we just can't change the way some things are.

In those defining moments, God gently whispers His loving command, "Surrender it to me!" For through these circumstances, God reminds us of who we are and who He is. We are the creation, but He is the Creator, and He is able to do all things well.

Remember, with God, all things are possible!

Take Him With You:

God can help you when
you surrender everything to Him.

It's Sin!

There is a way that appears to be right,
but in the end it leads to death.
- Proverbs 14:12

Whatever it may be, you just have to call it what it is: SIN! No gray area, just black and white! You can sugar-coat it, embrace it, and even tolerate it, but if God and the Bible calls it sin, it is sin and always will be sin!

Morality and immorality are not defined by man's changing attitudes and social customs. They are determined by the God of the universe, whose timeless truths, principles, and precepts cannot be ignored without dire consequences!

Take Him With You:

Only God decides what sin is,
and no man or law can change that!

Our Anchor

We have this hope as an anchor for the soul, firm and secure.
- Hebrews 6:19

We all need an anchor to cling to, that one thing that's immovable, unshakable, and steadfast, no matter the strength of the storm, difficulty, or circumstance we may be facing.

That anchor should always be the timeless truth that God never lies or makes a mistake!

No matter the challenge we may have before us, we can rest in the fact that it's always intended for our good by a God who loves us unconditionally and whose love never fails, falters, or changes.

Take Him With You:

For true peace and security,
your anchor in life must be in the unchanging God.

A Blessed Nation

Blessed is the nation whose God is the Lord.
- Psalm 33:12

"*The counsel of the LORD stands for ever, the thoughts of his heart to all generations. Blessed is the nation whose God is the LORD; and the people whom he hath chosen for his own inheritance.*" (Psalm 33:11, 12).

Praying that we will always be a Nation, a people whose God is the Lord. For when He is replaced in our everyday lives as Americans, then America, as we know her, will cease to exist!

Take Him With You:

The only hope for America is God's continued favor and blessing!

Ron Lambros

All We Need

May the God of hope fill you with all joy and peace as you trust in him, so that you may overflow with hope by the power of the Holy Spirit.
- Romans 15:13

Even deeply committed Christians can experience life at its worst. No one is immune. Even with years of faithfully walking with Christ, and a bag full of memorized Scriptures and promises, there are moments when even these don't seem to be enough to overcome life's challenges.

But when we have absolutely nothing else to draw upon except our feeble and frail faith, we will find that this is all we really need. And those are the exact moments when God will do His greatest work!

Take Him With You:

Even a small faith can overcome life's biggest challenges.

Tears Have a Language

The Lord is close to the brokenhearted
and saves those who are crushed in spirit.
- Psalm 34:18

The poetry of God is often written with stanzas of tears.

Life can be brutal and difficult to understand. We sometimes find ourselves heart-broken and weeping over its circumstances. But God cares and understands. Tears have a language all their own, and tear-filled eyes are not a sign of faltering faith, but of our humanity.

If God has put the love in your heart, He also understands its frailty and your tears.

Take Him With You:

God understands the language of your tears.

Obstacles

*"Not by might nor by power,
but by my Spirit," says the Lord Almighty.
- Zechariah 4:6*

Many frustrations in life center around a matter of focus. We see the hills and valleys, the forks in the road, the bumps and the delays—and we get angry and bitter because we feel they thwart our personal plans and ambitions.

But while we only see that which is directly before us, God sees "The Big Picture," and what we often perceive as obstacles are actually blessings in disguise that God uses to keep us on track and help us achieve His perfect plan for our lives.

Take Him With You:

**God often uses detours and obstacles
to keep you on the path He has for you.**

Too Big for God?

Jesus looked at them and said, "With man this is impossible, but with God all things are possible."
- Matthew 19:26

Have a problem or difficulty you think is too big for God?

Let's see: *Let there be light; Ask, Seek, Knock; Lazarus, come forth!; Peace, be still; It is written; In the beginning God; Your sins are forgiven; With God, all things are possible; Follow me; Feed my sheep; Be thou made whole; Only believe; Love one another; I am the way and the truth and the life; It is finished!*

Now, do you still think you have a problem that God can't handle?

Take Him With You:

**You will never have a problem
that's too big for God to handle!**

Ron Lambros

God's Been There

When Jesus saw her weeping, and the Jews who had come along with her also weeping, he was deeply moved in spirit and troubled. "Where have you laid him?" he asked. "Come and see, Lord," they replied. Jesus wept.
- John 11:33-35

We often feel that we're the only one in the world that's going through what we're going through, but God knows differently.

Are you struggling with gut-wrenching loss at a graveside? God's been there. Do you feel betrayed by those you love the most? God's been there. Have you given absolutely everything with truth, honesty, and love, only to have your intentions questioned or been treated like a piece of trash? God's been there, too.

In each and every circumstance of life, both good and bad, you're never alone. God's been there, and He understands!

Take Him With You:

God understands everything you're going through.
He's been there!

Clean and Forgiven

Let us draw near to God with a sincere heart and with the full assurance that faith brings, having our hearts sprinkled to cleanse us from a guilty conscience and having our bodies washed with pure water.
- Hebrews 10:22

Guilt and shame are like acid to spiritual power and strength. Who among us has not felt their sting or destruction? Yet our loving Heavenly Father has promised us a second chance if we but humbly ask. God loves a broken and repentant heart. When we stray from His grasp, we can become stained with sin. Coming to Him in brokenness and humility is all it takes to begin again, clean and forgiven, just as if we'd never sinned at all.

You have to love the God of the second chance!

Take Him With You:

God promises that you can begin again
if you ask Him for a second chance.

Ron Lambros

Don't Miss Him!

Holy, holy, holy is the Lord Almighty;
the whole earth is full of his glory.
- Isaiah 6:3

How often do we neglect, ignore, overlook, or simply miss the presence of our loving God? We often look for Him in the great rolling thunder when, more often than not, He comes in gentle whispers...in the soft cooing of a baby, through the touch of a loved one's hand, in the warm embrace of a trusted friend, in the pitter-patter of a sudden summer shower on a tin roof, or with the cool breath of an evening breeze on an Autumn night. Through hundreds of ways, God whispers, "I love you and I am always with you."

Don't miss Him or His presence as you go through this day. Open your eyes of faith and look for Him in the most simple of ways. The experience can be extraordinary and life-changing!

Take Him With You:

God reminds you in so many ways
that He's always there.

God's Attention

*For the eyes of the Lord are on the righteous
and his ears are attentive to their prayer.
- I Peter 3:12*

War. Famine. Pestilence. Drought. Natural disasters. You might feel that God has His hands full and would never care about your seemingly small, insignificant problem or concern. We all need to learn that when we approach God with our earnest, heartfelt cries, His full attention turns away from everything and everyone else and is fully focused on us. At that very moment, God cares more about you and your needs than anything or anyone else in the world. What a comfort and blessing!

Take Him With You:

When you pray, God is completely focused on you!

Ron Lambros

Sleeping Faith

...indeed, he who watches over Israel
will neither slumber nor sleep.
- Psalm 121:4

Like the disciples in the boat, we often find ourselves in the middle of a horrific storm, one that attacks the very core of our faith, only to look for God in it all and find Him, seemingly, sleeping in the back of the boat. And we get angry, bitter, and hurt because we feel that He just doesn't care about our plight.

The truth is, God has every storm in our life completely under control. In reality, we will find that it is our sleeping faith that's to blame for our fear and anguish.

God never slumbers nor sleeps.

Trust Him in every situation and circumstance!

Take Him With You:

Don't ever blame God for your lack of faith!

Seeing God's Miracles

You are the God who performs miracles;
you display your power among the peoples.
- Psalm 77:14

The problem with many Christians is not that their faith is sometimes weak or that they trust God only for the essentials of life. The problem with many Christians is that they go through their daily lives and never make room for God's miracles! When did God ever limit Himself or promise that He would do things just to a certain point or in a predictable way? Our faith needs to be stretched every day, and we must look for a miracle-working God to bless us when we least expect it!

Take Him With You:

You will see the miracles of God every day
if you simply look for them.

Answering the Question

When he had gone indoors, the blind men came to him, and he asked them, "Do you believe that I am able to do this?"
- Matthew 9:28

When all is said and done, the key to overcoming seemingly insurmountable objects and circumstances in life is how we answer the question Jesus posed to two blind men who sought His healing centuries ago: "*Do you believe that I am able to do this?*" No matter what trial you are facing or humanly impossible need you have, it all comes down to how you answer that one basic, yet powerful question. Do you really believe He can?

Remember, with God, ALL things are possible!

Take Him With You:

Do you have faith that believes God can do anything?

All You Need

...take up the shield of faith, with which you can extinguish all the flaming arrows of the evil one.
- Ephesians 6:16

Some days, your faith is all you've got. Fortunately, that's all you ever need!

Take Him With You:

You will find that your faith is all you ever need.

Ron Lambros

Hold Fast!

Be on your guard; stand firm in the faith;
be courageous; be strong.
- I Corinthians 16:13

Even the strongest believer has days of doubt, days of fear, and days of weakness. No one is immune to facing our own personal Red Sea impossibilities, Goliath-sized challenges, or Jericho wall improbabilities. In days like these, we must hold fast to the fact that God still has a staff, a stone, and a shout, and every obstacle, doubt, or fear we are facing is met head-on by the personal and all-powerful force of a God who loves us unconditionally and wants to help us in every way!

Take Him With You:

God can overcome any problem in your life,
no matter how impossible it seems.

The Litmus Test

Lord my God, I take refuge in you;
save and deliver me from all who pursue me.
- Psalm 7:1

It's in the personal moments of deep disappointment and discouragement that our faith is put to the litmus test. At those times, we must answer one specific question: Do I trust God or not? If not, we need to simply bend into a fetal position and waste away for the remainder of our lives. But if we do, we can face any hardship or circumstance with confidence, not in ourselves, but in the God who always knows what's best for us and promises to give it to us at His appointed time.

Take Him With You:

To be truly happy,
you must trust God with every facet of your life.

Ron Lambros

It All Boils Down to Perspective

Consider it pure joy, my brothers and sisters, whenever you face trials of many kinds, because you know that the testing of your faith produces perseverance.
Let perseverance finish its work so that you may be mature and complete, not lacking anything.
- James 1:2-4

Times of testing, no matter how large or small the degree, can be trying experiences for even the most seasoned believer. But it all boils down to perspective.

When pressed and pressured by circumstances, resist the urge to ask God to get you out of the situation you're in; instead, ask Him to reveal what He's trying to teach you while you're in the situation. Learning to see things from God's perspective is always a learning experience—one that will last a lifetime.

Take Him With You:

You learn so much when you see things from God's perspective.

The Faithfulness of God

Who is like you, Lord God Almighty?
You, Lord, are mighty, and your faithfulness surrounds you.
- Psalm 89:8

The faithfulness of God is not based on how you feel, how you see things, or how bad or good the circumstances are around you at any given moment. The faithfulness of God is born in the heart of God Himself and is based solely on the purest and deepest love no mortal man can possibly comprehend. It is uncompromising, it is eternal, and it is everlasting. His love and faithfulness never fail or falter. With that, any day, any circumstance, or any situation can be faced with hope and confidence, knowing God Himself is always working on your behalf.

Take Him With You:

**Rest in the knowledge that God
is always faithful to work on your behalf.**

Ron Lambros

The Siren Song of Sin

Be alert and of sober mind. Your enemy the devil prowls around like a roaring lion looking for someone to devour.
- I Peter 5:8

We all have our Achilles' heel—that weak link in our spiritual chain that Satan knows all too well. It could be anger, doubt, fear, sexual immorality, or any number of things which break our fellowship with God. We'll go days, months, or even years staying strong and faithful, avoiding that trap at all cost. Then, without warning or intent, we stumble, falter, and succumb to its siren song.

In those moments when Satan bogs us down in the quicksand of our weakness, God reminds us that failure is never final with His forgiveness. If you have stumbled or fallen in your faith, God stands ready to forgive, to restore, and to renew. He always does.

Now, forgive yourself!

Take Him With You:

**When you fall into sin's pit,
accept the rescue of God's forgiveness.**

He Will Carry It

My eyes are on all their ways; they are not hidden from me,
nor is their sin concealed from my eyes.
- Jeremiah 16:17

Don't fool yourself! God knows you better than you know yourself. That hidden sin? He knows about it. Those hateful thoughts? He knows them, too. That hidden bitterness, anger, doubt, and fear? He knows them all and more. Does He condemn or punish? No, He forgives and offers rest. *"Come unto me all who are burdened and loaded down with the weight of life, and I will give you rest."* God will not only lighten your load, He will lift it completely and carry it for you.

God's shoulders are big, and in our weakness, He is strong!

Take Him With You:

God wants to forgive the burden
of your sin and give you rest.

Ron Lambros

The Language of God

May the Lord direct your hearts
into God's love and Christ's perseverance.
- II Thessalonians 3:5

The language of God. No matter the trial, no matter the circumstance, no matter the depth of sin, God always speaks the language of love and forgiveness.

Said something you swore you would never say? Did something you promised you would never do? Facing something you've never faced before? Listen to the language of God. Listen to His gentle whisper or thundering command, but listen. When you hear His words and obey, your heart will be clean, your sin forgiven, your faith strengthened, and your fellowship restored.

God's language is always unconditional love, and He's speaking to you today.

Take Him With You:

God always speaks to you with the language of perfect love and forgiveness.

The One True Source

Humble yourselves, therefore, under God's mighty hand,
that he may lift you up in due time.
- I Peter 5:6

There are moments in the life of every believer when the burdens, doubts, and fears we are forced to face literally strip us to our very core, where everyone and everything we ever believed in seems improbable or untrue, leaving us vulnerable and floundering in our faith. It is in these moments that our faith is defined and our beliefs are refined, and we cling to the one true Source of power and strength to see us through.

When we are completely empty of self, it is then that God shows His greatest love and capacity to solve any situation, problem, or circumstance that we perceive as impossible.

He IS our strength!

Take Him With You:

God wants you to depend on His strength
when your faith is weak.

Ron Lambros

The Language of the Heart

And he who searches our hearts knows the mind of the Spirit, because the Spirit intercedes for God's people in accordance with the will of God.
- Romans 8:27

There are some days in the life of every believer when there are simply no spoken words that can adequately express the depth of our grief, discouragement, disappointment, sorrow, fear, depression, frustration, heartbreak, or doubt. They simply won't come. The mouth is silent while the tears flow, and the sighs, moans, and groans we utter become the language of our hearts.

But God knows and understands even the heart that never speaks. He understands the groans, the moans, and the tears, and He embraces every one with the same compassion and caring as the most eloquent prayer ever uttered.

Never doubt that God cares and understands when there are simply no words to say. He does—and He always will!

Take Him With You:

God hears and understands every word you never say.

Words

For I have kept the ways of the Lord;
I am not guilty of turning from my God.
- Psalm 18:21

The most powerful weapon known to man is the spoken word. In the right hands, it has the power to change lives for the better, to pass down godly traditions and beliefs, and to insure that our future generations have all that is good and wholesome which they, in turn, will continue to pass down long after we are gone. Sadly, in the wrong hands, words can be used for evil, their venom and poison spreading like a plague, doing nothing but destroying those who hear them.

Give no heed to the words of a fool! His words are empty and lifeless, like his soul. One day, his words will cease, and the only thing he will be remembered for is the vile filth he openly and proudly shared with little regard for the consequences. Pity this man, for he has never truly lived and will never know true joy or happiness, for his heart is dead and void of any feeling.

Take Him With You:

Your words can be used for good or evil.
Use them wisely.

Ron Lambros

Mustard Seed Faith

He said to his disciples, "Why are you so afraid?
Do you still have no faith?"
- Mark 4:40

There are definable moments in each of our lives that boil down to nothing more than simply trusting God—moments that test the very core of our faith to the breaking point, stripping us of every comfort and security we've ever known. Moments where every Scripture we've ever memorized seems inadequate, every sermon we've ever heard seems lacking in power, every prayer we've ever uttered feels useless. These are "mustard seed moments," when the bare essence of our faith is as small as it can be. Yet it is at these very moments that God proves to us that that is all the faith we truly ever need.

God sometimes takes us to the breaking point just to prove that it all boils down to you and Him, and that our faith, no matter how small, is all that matters!

Take Him With You:

Your faith, no matter how small,
is all you really ever need.

God Steps In

May your hand be ready to help me,
for I have chosen your precepts.
- Psalm 119:173

You finally came to it. That one situation or circumstance that has broken your heart, shaken your security and well-being to its very core, or brought more doubt, fear, and uncertainty than you've ever experienced in your life. No amount of praying will overcome it. No amount of pleading to God will satisfy it. No measure of pounding your fists will conquer it.

And that's when it happens: God steps in.

For when you come to the end of yourself and have done all you can with all the human strength and determination you can muster, God shows you that He alone can do that which you deem impossible. God is boundless in His capabilities, timeless in His faithfulness, and limitless in His desire to help you.

Quit fighting in your own strength and give it over to God. He alone can meet your every need, just as He promised He would!

Take Him With You:

Quit fighting in your own strength
and give your impossibilities to God!

Ron Lambros

God Takes Over

I am with you and will watch over you wherever you go, and I will bring you back to this land. I will not leave you until I have done what I promised you.
- Genesis 28:15

There are moments when you wake to simply feel nothing. Life, with all of its challenges and circumstances, makes you numb and void of any thought or feeling. You attempt to pray, but you're unable to verbalize what your heart is screaming. You cannot articulate what you are going through. You only know that you feel empty and cannot focus on the next step to take.

This is the critical moment when you must simply be still and let God take over, for many times, it is He who brings us to the end of ourselves to show Himself strong on our behalf. Do not think for one moment that just because you don't understand what you're going through or why you feel the way you do, that He doesn't. As your Creator, He knows every facet of your being and reminds you that you are *fearfully and wonderfully made.*

Do not fear or fight your emptiness; rather, embrace His fullness and presence, through faith, in your circumstance.

Take Him With You:

Embrace God's presence when you feel empty or afraid.

Come!

You will make known to me the path of life;
you will fill me with joy in your presence,
with eternal pleasures at your right hand.
- Psalm 16:11

Some days, we cannot sense God's presence. We feel alone, abandoned, and afraid. We are confused by His promise that He would never leave us nor forsake us, yet we do not sense that He is near.

Other times, we can feel His very essence around us. We feel that we can almost reach out and touch Him and feel Him and smell His Heavenly aroma. Those are the special moments we are given as His children—the moments we have when we sense His very Being among us. And it is those very moments that assure us that, even when we can't sense that He is near, He is as ever-present as in those moments of grandeur when we can almost touch Him and sense His very presence.

Take His hand and walk with Him today. The garden path is cool, and He bids you, "Come!"

Take Him With You:

God is always with you
whether you sense His presence or not.

Priorities

If that is how God clothes the grass of the field, which is here today, and tomorrow is thrown into the fire, how much more will he clothe you—you of little faith! And do not set your heart on what you will eat or drink; do not worry about it. For the pagan world runs after all such things, and your Father knows that you need them. But seek his kingdom, and these things will be given to you as well.
- Luke 12:28-31

There are some days when you're simply not happy. There's no rhyme or reason to this unhappiness, no specific cause. You're simply suffering from "the blues." You have a great family, great job, enough money to meet your needs, and by all standards, have every reason to feel blessed and fortunate. And you do, but you're just not happy. The joy just isn't there.

These are the times that you must realize that God is often at work. He is stripping you to the bare bones of your faith and making you look at what's important—really important—in your life. He wants you to realize that life has absolutely nothing to do with your job, your family, the money you make, or anything else you put before Him! God is a jealous God, and sometimes, He will remind us that our happiness should never be identified with the *things* of this world. Our happiness should be based on our salvation, on an intimate relationship with the God who loves us unconditionally and never breaks a promise, and the hope and assurance of eternity. Anything else is second-best.

Are you unhappy today? Explore your priorities. What is God whispering in your heart at this very moment?

Take Him With You:

**True happiness is found in your
personal relationship with Jesus Christ.**

Anger

Everyone should be quick to listen, slow to speak and slow to become angry, because human anger does not produce the righteousness that God desires.
- James 1:19, 20

Anger can be a cancer to the soul and spirit, lying dormant deep within us until a person or event brings it spewing forth. We must remember that anger does not honor God and has no place in the life of the believer. Even though it is often justified and our human emotions erupt with it, we must not sin when influenced by its vile nature.

God wants us to live our lives with love, power, and a sound mind. Anger creates a tempest within the heart and confusion within the mind. We rage against it and all-too-often succumb to its evil nature. When that occurs, immediately seek God's forgiveness and pray for a peaceful heart and mind to return.

Anger and peace are spiritual oil and water: they can never be mixed together. With God's strength, anger can be overcome, so seek peace at all times.

Take Him With You:

Your uncontrolled anger will always lead to spiritual disaster.

Your Red Sea

The Lord will fight for you; you need only to be still.
- Exodus 14:14

I have stood before my own Red Sea—that circumstance, problem, challenge, or situation when I've cried out to God, "What do I do now? This sea before me is immovable, impassable, and impossible!"

In a gentle, quiet whisper, God replied, "Be still!"

At that very moment, I released every doubt, every fear, and every question, and simply stood, patiently waiting for God to move as He promised me He would.

Slowly, the sea began to move. A ripple at first, then a roaring and crashing of waves, until the sea parted, and God made a way for me through my difficulty.

Never doubt that God is moving in your circumstance. His provision is sometimes a ripple and sometimes a roaring of waves, but the answer will come. Let your faith release its doubt and fear, standing firmly on His promise that He will walk with you through every problem and difficulty you may face in your life!

Be still! The way is coming! And God promises you won't need swimming lessons!

Take Him With You:

Make sure your faith is standing on
God's promises and not your circumstances.

"I Trust You, Jesus!"

I will say of the Lord, "He is my refuge and my fortress,
my God, in whom I trust."
- Psalm 91:2

Many days begin with anxiety, frustration, and fear. You find that the baggage you went to bed with is still weighing heavily on your emotions, and you simply don't know what to do. The very people that you admired, loved, respected, and supported have disappointed or abandoned you. You feel used, bewildered, and at a loss for words.

It is then that you softly whisper, "I trust you, Jesus!"

As you do, you feel the weight begin to lift, and soon you find yourself freed from the burden that weighed you down in the first place.

Some days your faith is all you have. Fortunately, it's all you ever need!

Take Him With You:

Trust Jesus with every area of your life.
He will never fail you.

Ron Lambros

Time

...for I delight in your commands because I love them.
I reach out for your commands, which I love,
that I may meditate on your decrees.
- Psalm 119:47, 48

There are many ways to worship God. We can do it through prayer, singing, reading His Word, or recognizing His presence all around us every day, just to name a few. But the greatest way to worship God is with our time. T-I-M-E...mankind's greatest commodity, yet most squandered gift.

To truly worship God, we must set aside the hustle-and-bustle of pressing engagements, hurried schedules, and electronic leashes, and simply meditate daily with the Creator of the universe.

God longs for us to spend time with Him, and it is only by doing so that God will speak to our hearts as He desires to do, and will impart to us His perfect will and way for our lives.

Take Him With You:

You must invest time with God
every day to truly know and trust Him.

God of the Infinite

"I am the Alpha and the Omega," says the Lord God,
"who is, and who was, and who is to come, the Almighty."
- Revelation 1:8

All too often, we think of God as a Supreme Being who possesses our own human frailties and shortcomings. We could not be more wrong! Our God is a perfect God who has always been, a God who is not limited by time or space, and a God whose infinite wisdom is so great that we cannot begin to fathom its depth or measure.

When going to God with your finite problems and circumstances, approach Him as a Holy God of the infinite who knew your name before time began, who loves you unconditionally, and who always has your best interest at heart.

Take Him With You:

**Always remember,
God is infinite and perfect, and you are not.**

Ron Lambros

Waiting on God

I wait for the Lord, my whole being waits,
and in his word I put my hope.
- Psalm 130:5

Waiting is never fun. We don't like it, and it's never easy. We wait in lines, at traffic lights, or when we're put on hold during phone conversations. We tap our feet, strum our fingers, and quietly fume because things are not moving as quickly as we feel they should.

And it's especially difficult when we're waiting on God to meet our needs or answer our prayers. We often feel angry and frustrated because we feel He should act immediately and let us get on with our lives.

But always remember, it's in the wait that endurance, patience, character, and hope are formed and molded. Don't allow the wait to rob you of seeing God for who He truly is. Many times, the answer to our prayer is not God's greatest gift to us at all. Instead, it's seeing the character and nature of a holy and righteous God in His purest form. And it's finding that His faithfulness and unconditional love were there all the time.

Take Him With You:

The faithfulness of God is always there, even in the wait.

Only Love

Be merciful, just as your Father is merciful.
- Luke 6:36

Parenting is never easy. We go from teaching life's basics to life's necessities in a matter of a few years. Then we release our children into the world hoping for perfection and a mistake-free life. We are elated by their successes and grieve at their failures. We rejoice with their accomplishments and are saddened when they become prodigals. But we love them none-the-less. And God is no different. God, a perfect Father, has imperfect children, yet He loves each one of us unconditionally. We owe our children the same mercy, respect, and grace that we have received from Him. No excuses, no resentment...only love.

Take Him With You:

**You must love your children
as God loves His...unconditionally.**

Ron Lambros

Just as You Are

...you are precious and honored in my sight,
and because I love you...
- Isaiah 43:4

Some days, it seems that it just doesn't pay to get out of bed. You're maligned, misunderstood, and unappreciated by the world around you, even with your best efforts.

Isn't it comforting to know that God created you and loves you just like you are, and that nothing you can do will ever cause Him to love you any more or any less?

Forget the world and all its naysayers. Go boldly into the day knowing that there's a God who values you, paves the way for you, and is cheering you on!

Take Him With You:

God loves you just the way you are.

Embrace Your Gift

The thief comes only to steal and kill and destroy;
I have come that they may have life, and have it to the full.
- John 10:10

God has a plan for your life. He made it long before He even created you. He knows the hows, whats, whys, whens, and wheres of that plan, and knows its beginning and its end. You may not like it or always agree with it, but if you embrace it as a very special gift, you will find your life richer and fuller for trusting Him and believing that He always knows what He's doing for your good and His glory.

God's plan is meant to prosper you and not harm you, and He made it especially for you to give you hope and a future.

Now, what can be better than that?

Take Him With You:

Embrace God's plan for your life as a gift.
He knows what He's doing.

Ron Lambros

A Matter of Faith

...being strengthened with all power according to his glorious might so that you may have great endurance and patience, and giving joyful thanks to the Father, who has qualified you to share in the inheritance of his holy people in the kingdom of light.
- Colossians 1:11, 12

Sometimes, the most gut-wrenching decisions you ever have to make are really the blessings of God in disguise. It all comes down to a matter of faith and trust in the One who controls it all.

Take Him With You:

Never confuse your difficulties with God's blessings!

The Measure of Our Trust

Blessed is the one who perseveres under trial because, having stood the test, that person will receive the crown of life that the Lord has promised to those who love him.
- James 1:12

Sometimes, fully trusting God is the most difficult thing to do. The raw emotion, grief, pain, and confusion found in many of life's moments cause us to pause and question why a loving God would ever let them happen.

It's in those unbelievably life-shattering moments that God sometimes asks us if we trust Him enough to thank Him even when it's difficult to do, or when we may never fully understand or know the reason why. How we answer that question will always reflect the depth of our faith and the measure of our trust in Him.

Take Him With You:

Trusting God when you don't understand is difficult, but necessary.

Ron Lambros

Never Alone

So do not fear, for I am with you; do not be dismayed, for I am your God. I will strengthen you and help you; I will uphold you with my righteous right hand.
- Isaiah 41:10

Life isn't always easy. We have good days and bad days, and the combination of the two often fuels our mood, attitude, and faith. When things are good, we think God is smiling and walking close to us. When they are bad, we often feel He is distant and uncaring.

We must learn that no matter how good or bad things are, God is always with us. He is walking before us to lead us, behind us to protect us, beside us to support us, and within us to guide, comfort, and encourage us.

God never changes, and He never leaves us alone!

Take Him With You:

God never changes, and He will never leave you alone!

His Pursuit

When I said, "My foot is slipping," your unfailing love, Lord,
supported me. When anxiety was great within me, your
consolation brought me joy.
- Psalm 94:18, 19

Why do so many of us struggle with the fact that God loves us unconditionally, and that no matter how good or bad we are, He'll never stop loving us? God is the only one who never gives up on us, never abandons us, never forgets about us or ceases to care about us. We can never go anywhere without His merciful and compassionate pursuit.

Think you're unlovable and that nobody cares about you? Pause, and always remember that God does, and He always will!

Take Him With You:

Never doubt that God always loves you
and He always will.

Ron Lambros

How God Sees Us

I delight greatly in the Lord; my soul rejoices in my God. For he has clothed me with garments of salvation and arrayed me in a robe of his righteousness, as a bridegroom adorns his head like a priest, and as a bride adorns herself with her jewels.
- Isaiah 61:10

What do you see when you look at yourself in the mirror? If you're honest, along with the "good," you'll also see the "bad." After all, who among us is totally satisfied with ourselves? Even those who project the most confident image are often the most insecure, with feelings of failure or a lack of self-esteem.

As a child of God, we must look at ourselves in truth: we are the offspring of a God who loves us unconditionally, who gave Himself sacrificially for us, and when He looks at us, He doesn't see us for who we think we are, but for who He thinks we are—His child, clothed in His righteousness.

Nothing we can possibly project in the mirror can match how God sees each of us. Rest in that thought and perspective today, and be encouraged!

Take Him With You:

God always sees you through His eyes, not yours.

All My Love, Jesus

God's Victory

*He will cover you with his feathers,
and under his wings you will find refuge; his faithfulness will
be your shield and rampart. You will not fear the terror of
night, nor the arrow that flies by day...*
- Psalm 91:4, 5

9/11. Car bombings. Terrorism. Mass murders. Through it all, with all the turmoil and uncertainty, the fear and dread of the unknown, God remains steadfast, unmovable, and always in control.

When the world and mankind are at their worst, God is at His best. He is our constant source of strength and peace that no bomb can rattle or terrorist attack can shake. He may not get the headlines, but He always gets the glory! Satan may have his day, but God's victory will be eternal and complete!

Rest in Him!

Take Him With You:

When your world is at its worst, God is at His best!

Patience

The Lord is slow to anger, abounding in love and forgiving sin and rebellion. Yet he does not leave the guilty unpunished...
- Numbers 14:18

Don't ever mistake God's patience for His permission!

Take Him With You:

Always weigh your actions
and decisions based on the Word of God.

Quench Your Thirst

As the deer pants for streams of water,
so my soul pants for you, my God.
- Psalm 42:1

My wife, Bridget, has a beautiful collection of flowers on our deck. On a hot, sunny day, those flowers wither and bow low from lack of water. So it is with our heart, mind, soul, and spirit. In times of deep despair, anguish, and need, we long for the refreshing presence of our God. Scripture says it best in Psalm 42:1: *"As the deer pants for streams of water, so my soul pants for you, my God."* Quench all that your soul thirsts for today. Draw near to Him and experience His nourishment and life-sustaining Spirit.

Take Him With You:

When life has you in the desert,
quench your thirst with God!

The Bible

*All Scripture is God-breathed and is useful for teaching,
rebuking, correcting and training in righteousness,
so that the servant of God may be thoroughly
equipped for every good work.*
- II Timothy 3:16, 17

The Bible is God's gift, His guidebook, for our lives. No one will ever be so smart that they don't need its wisdom, never get so strong that they don't need its power, and will never be so successful that they don't need its daily guidance and direction.

No one!

Take Him With You:

**The Bible is all you need for wisdom,
strength, and success in life.**

Christian Resolve

We are hard pressed on every side, but not crushed; perplexed, but not in despair; persecuted, but not abandoned; struck down, but not destroyed.
- II Corinthians 4:8, 9

There are times of trouble in the life of every believer. It's simply a part of daily life. The struggle comes, and we face it with a faith and trust in God that years of facing other problems have taught us. But then there are those times when an avalanche of heartache and grief challenges us, driving us to our knees and causing us to beg God for mercy and grace. These are those special times of testing that can make-or-break our Christian resolve. In those moments of being overwhelmed by a bombardment of circumstances, we must firmly plant our feet and face each one with the immutable truth and belief in the sovereignty of God. His wisdom is far beyond our own, and His intellect is more than we can fathom.

Always remember, if His love and caring for us allowed Him to send Jesus to the cross to die for us, we must know He cares enough to see us through whatever difficulty or challenge we may be facing. You may question God's reasons, but never question His unconditional love or His heart.

Take Him With You:

You can face any difficulty
if you have faith in the sovereignty of God.

Where True Faith Begins

Your faithfulness continues through all generations...
- Psalm 119:90

It finally happens. That moment, situation, or circumstance in your life that rocks you to the very foundation of your faith, and every sermon you ever heard, every Scripture you ever memorized, every prayer you ever uttered, just doesn't seem to be enough to see you through this time. Your spirit is crushed beyond belief, and your anxiety, worry, doubt, and fear have you paralyzed.

Always remember that when you come to the end of yourself—that is where true faith begins! Hold fast to the promises of God and the memories of past spiritual battles won. He hasn't changed, and His Word and promises are still true today.

Faithful He has always been and faithful He will always be!

Take Him With You:

When new trials come,
remember what God's already brought you through.

Ron Lambros

A Sin Issue

Righteousness exalts a nation, but sin condemns any people.
- Proverbs 14:34

America is facing serious issues and civil unrest. The world is facing terrorism with its unspeakable brutality and threats. So much violence and upheaval, hatred, and bitterness. But these—and every other problem or situation that causes our hearts to shudder and fear—are not race issues, not terrorism issues, not gun violence issues, and are not we-vs.-them issues. At their very core, you'll find that all of these atrocities are a SIN issue, and no authority or legislation on earth can stop it or cure it. It all begins with each of us coming to God with broken and repentant hearts, for only Almighty God Himself can bring true peace to our world, our Nation, and our people.

I pray that He will do it and that He will do it soon!

Take Him With You:

Our world is plagued by a sin issue,
and its only cure can come from God alone.

On the Line

Love the Lord your God and keep his requirements,
his decrees, his laws and his commands always.
- Deuteronomy 11:1

Sometimes, God asks you to do something so profound, so out of the ordinary, so challenging, that your faith shudders, and your belief is strained. Like Abraham and Isaac, your trust in the guidance and instruction of God is put to the test: it's your will vs. obedience to God.

In moments like these, all that you trust and believe is put on the line. Will you or won't you trust God? Your decision could have life-changing, even eternal, consequences.

Trust and obey!

Take Him With You:

Always be obedient and trust God,
even when you don't agree or understand.

Ron Lambros

Your Life Matters

For we are God's handiwork, created in Christ Jesus to do good works, which God prepared in advance for us to do.
- Ephesians 2:10

Long before the breath of God was felt throughout the vastness of time and space, long before the wave of His mighty hand began to form matter out of nothing, and long before the gentle thunder of His voice spoke the worlds, the planets, and the universe into existence, God knew your name. He numbered the hairs on your head and developed His exact plan and purpose for your life.

If you don't think your life matters or that you don't make a difference, then stop and realize that God thinks differently. You are loved by Him and are an important piece of His puzzle.

Don't cheat yourself or God out of fulfilling the plan He has for you. He's done His part, and now He's depending on you to do yours!

Take Him With You:

God has a plan and purpose for your life.
Do your part to make it happen.

All My Love, Jesus

Checkmate!

Many are the plans in a person's heart,
but it is the Lord's purpose that prevails.
- Proverbs 19:21

Life is a lot like a chess match. On one side of the game board is your life. On the other side are all the challenges, trials, heartaches, and obstacles you will face. Each piece of your life has a distinct and specific purpose. When challenges come, they are met with the piece of your life best suited for the task. Some trials and heartaches require bigger pieces with greater power, strength, and capabilities. And with each move of each piece, each obstacle is met with victory in mind.

The greatest decision you will ever face when you sit down at the chessboard of life is whether you will control the pieces or whether you will allow God to control them.

With your limited knowledge and ability, no matter how great, you are moving each piece one at a time, matching life moment-for-moment. God is the Grand Master and sees the total content of your life, and every move He makes is made with His infinite future moves already planned and in place. God knows what He's doing, He knows His complete and total plan for your life, and He alone will match life move-for-move, but always with total victory in mind. Let the Grand

Master take control of your life. Allow Him to strategically and perfectly move each piece, each facet of it, until He has completed the task and assignment He has for you. You may feel like a Pawn from time to time and a King at other times. Either way, God assures you of a victorious checkmate each and every time you place your life in the hands of the Grand Master.

Take Him With You:

Always trust the moves of God in your life, both large and small.

Just Like He Planned

What no eye has seen, what no ear has heard,
and what no human mind has conceived—
the things God has prepared for those who love him...
- I Corinthians 2:9

A person's life is not defined by one victory or one failure. It is a culmination of thousands of decisions, both large and small, good and bad, right and wrong, that a person makes in their lifetime.

The greatest promise we have is that God personally guarantees us that a life lived for Him will always turn out as He has planned, and that eternity with Him will be something that we cannot begin to fathom, imagine, or even comprehend.

Take Him With You:

If you live for Him,
God's plan for your life will be unimaginable.

Ron Lambros

Embrace the New

See, I am doing a new thing! Now it springs up; do you not perceive it? I am making a way in the wilderness and streams in the wasteland.
- Isaiah 43:19

"To everything there is a season, and a time to every purpose under the heaven..." (Ecclesiastes 3:1).

We all come to crossroads in our lives that define the closing of one chapter and the beginning of a new one. It is comforting to know that, as a child of God, each new chapter was written long before time and space existed, before a single breeze blew against the landscape of nothingness. This new chapter was born in the heart of God Himself, and was written with a quill of love, purpose, and perfection.

It is often difficult and painful to leave the past, but it is so much more exciting to embrace the perfect future plan and will of God for our lives, going forward in faith, and trusting in the One who knows the beginning from the end and every moment in-between.

The page is turning. Embrace it!

Take Him With You:

Trusting God often means change, but never outside His plan for your life.

Nothing is Greater Than God!

You, dear children, are from God and have overcome them,
because the one who is in you is greater
than the one who is in the world.
- I John 4:4

No matter what you think or how you feel, no matter how dire or difficult the circumstance or situation, no matter the pain or the bitterness that is raging within you...absolutely nothing that anyone can ever say or do to you is greater than the power, promises, provision, and principles of Almighty God! Absolutely nothing!

Now start living like it!

Take Him With You:

Nothing in your life is greater
or more powerful than Almighty God!

Ron Lambros

Remembering God's Goodness

Remember the wonders he has done,
his miracles, and the judgments he pronounced...
- Psalm 105:5

No one can possibly look to the promises of a New Year or even a new day without remembering the goodness of God in the past. He is the same yesterday, today, and forever, and His mercies are new every morning. As the old hymn says: *Great is thy faithfulness, O God my Father; There is no shadow of turning with thee; Thou changest not, Thy compassions; they fail not; As Thou hast been, thou forever will be...Strength for today and bright hope for tomorrow, Blessings all mine, with ten thousand beside!* (Thomas O. Chisholm)

Happy New Year!

Take Him With You:

As you begin this New Year,
thank God for His faithfulness.

Stay True to Yourself

Blessed are the peacemakers,
for they will be called children of God.
- Matthew 5:9

Being misunderstood or controversial is never easy. Being the one accused of eliciting unrest or stirring up emotions of bitterness and hatred is difficult. Being the one who stands firmly on their principles and beliefs at all costs is either appreciated or detested. But being true to yourself—unwavering, uncompromising, even though it goes against the tide of public opinion—must be admired and respected.

Always stay true to yourself and to your convictions. It's the only way to successfully live the life that God intends for you to enjoy.

Take Him With You:

Always stay true to yourself
and to your God-given convictions.

Ron Lambros

God's Valentine Card

*For God so loved the world that he gave his one
and only Son, that whoever believes in
him shall not perish but have eternal life.*
- John 3:16

The most beautiful Valentine's Day card didn't come from Hallmark. It was lovingly and personally designed by God Himself. It had no frilly lace, satin hearts, or pretty ribbons. On its cover, a blood-stained Roman cross, three rusty spikes, and a crown of thorns; on the inside, eight life-changing words: "I love you and did this for you."

I hope you've received God's special gift for you. An empty tomb beats candy and roses any day!

Take Him With You:

God's greatest act of love is the cross of Jesus Christ.

Godly Citizenry

Let everyone be subject to the governing authorities, for there is no authority except that which God has established. The authorities that exist have been established by God.
- Romans 13:1

America has been blessed with godly founders and leaders who sought to establish and govern this Nation on the principles and precepts of Almighty God. The Judeo-Christian ethic has been the plumb-bob for our foundational structure and well-being as a Country, though many times, we struggled to maintain that balance and priority.

Whatever your political slant or party, as believers, we are to stay true to our convictions while following and respecting our Country's leadership. Each one has been placed in a position of authority by God Himself, and we must, therefore, be involved citizens, supportive of our governing authorities, while at the same time maintaining our personal, spiritual convictions which supersede political or party lines.

Jesus said, *"Render to Caesar the things that are Caesar's; and to God the things that are God's."* (Matthew 22:21). Be subject to earthly governmental authority, yes, but always maintain your spiritual convictions and the principles and precepts God has given you. We must be part of a godly citizenry, but never at the cost of disrespecting or disregarding those in authority over us.

Take Him With You:

Acknowledge and **respect those in authority.**
They are God's choice.

The Shadow of the Cross

When he came near the place where the road goes down the Mount of Olives, the whole crowd of disciples began joyfully to praise God in loud voices for all the miracles they had seen: "Blessed is the king who comes in the name of the Lord!" "Peace in heaven and glory in the highest!"
- Luke 19:37, 38

A day had passed since Jesus made His entry into Jerusalem. The people had cheered and waved palm fronds before Him, all while the religious leaders plotted against Him. Judas pondered thoughts of betrayal, while Jesus planned His final meal with His disciples. Sorrow gripped His heart. His three-year ministry was coming to an end, as was His very life. And with every breath he took, the shadow of the cross grew larger.

Take Him With You:

Always remember that Jesus knew that the cross was why He came!

Ron Lambros

Complete Sacrifice

When the hour came, Jesus and his apostles reclined at the table. And he said to them, "I have eagerly desired to eat this Passover with you before I suffer. For I tell you, I will not eat it again until it finds fulfillment in the kingdom of God."
- Luke 22:14-16

The dining area was prepared for the Passover Feast...just Jesus and His disciples one last time for one last meal together. So much more to do, so much more to teach them. Where to begin.

In humble fashion, He washed their feet, even the feet of the one who had betrayed Him. The hands that cupped the water for washing feet would soon be pierced by rusty spikes.

Is there any greater act of obedience than complete sacrifice?

Take Him With You:

Jesus is your example of perfect love, obedience, and sacrifice!

Betrayal

While he was still speaking a crowd came up, and the man
who was called Judas, one of the Twelve, was leading them.
He approached Jesus to kiss him, but Jesus asked him,
"Judas, are you betraying the Son of Man with a kiss?"
- Luke 22:47, 48

He did it with a kiss. Judas in the Garden and the ultimate betrayal was accomplished. Today, millions of hearts feel the very same pain and hurt of betrayal. Hearts lie bruised and battered by broken vows, broken promises, and broken trusts. And no one is immune to its vile effects.

Isn't it good to know that, at Easter and every day, we have Someone we can always trust, never lose faith in, and Who loves us unconditionally, no matter the circumstance? And we can always trust Him, not just for today, not just for the moment, but for eternity!

Take Him With You:

If you have been betrayed,
trust Jesus for healing and understanding!

Ron Lambros

You Were on His Mind

Then the whole assembly rose and led him off to Pilate. So Pilate asked Jesus, "Are you the king of the Jews?"
"You have said so," Jesus replied.
Then Pilate announced to the chief priests and the crowd, "I find no basis for a charge against this man." But they insisted...
- Luke 23:1; 3-5

Tonight as we sleep, centuries ago, Jesus was in the Garden. There were drops of blood, a resignation of the will, Roman soldiers, and a pucker from Judas. Soon, He'd be mocked and face a Roman kangaroo court. While insults and false accusations were being hurled, a leather whip was being prepared, and in the distance, the sawing of timbers for a cross.

And all that was on His mind at that very moment was you and me.

Take Him With You:

If you ever feel unimportant,
remember that Jesus went to the cross for you!

Eden's Sin

When they came to the place called the Skull, they crucified him there, along with the criminals—one on his right, the other on his left. Jesus said, "Father, forgive them, for they do not know what they are doing."
- Luke 23:33, 34

The trial and beating were over, and He now struggled under the weight of the wooden beam. It dug splinters deep into His back. Spit and sweat stung His wounds. Soon, He would be staked to the timbers of a Roman cross, hanging in the heat of the day by three rusty spikes. Satan would hiss a laugh of approval while God waited for the sin to pass and His plan to be complete. Eden's sin would finally be made right, and our eternity would, once again, be restored.

Take Him With You:

Be encouraged that no man can ever thwart the plans and purposes of God!

Ron Lambros

Just a Day Away

The women who had come with Jesus from
Galilee followed Joseph and saw the tomb
and how his body was laid in it. Then they went home and
prepared spices and perfumes. But they rested on the
Sabbath in obedience to the commandment.
- Luke 23:55, 56

All was fairly quiet now. The crucifixion was over, and Jesus' body was placed in a borrowed tomb which was sealed and guarded. The disciples scattered, aftershocks rumbled, and the priests were trying to figure out how to repair the curtain in the Holy of Holies. Satan was celebrating while God simply smiled and waited. God's plans and prophesies were almost complete.

Jesus was dead, but Sunday was just a day away.

Take Him With You:

You must always walk by faith, not by sight!

He Is Risen!

...suddenly two men in clothes that gleamed like lightning stood beside them. In their fright the women bowed down with their faces to the ground, but the men said to them, "Why do you look for the living among the dead? He is not here; he has risen!"
- Luke 24:4-6

Mary made her way up the path in the morning dew. She hadn't slept much since the crucifixion, and she didn't know what she'd find when she got to the tomb. She just knew she had to go.

When she got there, the massive stone that once sealed the entrance was rolled away and the tomb itself was empty, except for the neatly folded burial clothes of Jesus.

Then she heard the words that shook eternity forever:

"He is not here; He has risen!"
May these same words echo in our hearts today and always.

Happy Easter!

Take Him With You:
**Celebrate today and every day that
Jesus Christ is your living and risen Savior!**

Ron Lambros

He Did It for You

...I live by faith in the Son of God,
who loved me and gave himself for me.
- Galatians 2:20

There are many things to be thankful for at Easter: the loving plan of God for the redemption of Man, the ultimate sacrifice of the Son, and the resurrection of a risen Savior.

But never forget that one of the most incredible things about Easter is the fact that if you were the only person on the face of the earth, Jesus would have still come and died for you!

What a humbling thought, and what a great God we serve!

Take Him With You:

The glory and joy of Easter is that
Jesus is risen, and He did it for you!

All My Love, Jesus

Your Gethsemane

Dear friends, do not be surprised at the fiery ordeal that has come on you to test you, as though something strange were happening to you. But rejoice inasmuch as you participate in the sufferings of Christ, so that you may be overjoyed when his glory is revealed. However, if you suffer as a Christian, do not be ashamed, but praise God that you bear that name.
- I Peter 4:12, 13; 16

Following God's will isn't always easy or pleasant. Many times, it will lead you through your own personal Garden of Gethsemane, a time of great struggle, pain, and anguish, before the full accomplishment of all God has planned for your life is realized with complete and total obedience and surrender.

As you follow God, always seek to do as He leads, but be prepared for the trials and testing that may soon follow. Through it all, He will be glorified, and you will succeed.

Take Him With You:

You will face trials as you follow God's plan for your life, but stay faithful.

Ron Lambros

Prayer

If my people, who are called by my name, will humble themselves and pray and seek my face and turn from their wicked ways, then I will hear from heaven, and I will forgive their sin and will heal their land.
- II Chronicles 7:14

"If my people, who are called by my name, will humble themselves and pray and seek my face and turn from their wicked ways, then I will hear from heaven, and I will forgive their sin and will heal their land." - II Chronicles 7:14.

Honoring God on this National Day of Prayer, for He alone is not only worthy of our prayer and praise, but He is our only hope, security, and sufficiency as a Nation and as a people.

Take Him With You:
**Our only hope as a Nation
and people is repentance and God's favor!**

Take Time to Pray

Do not be anxious about anything, but in every situation, by prayer and petition, with thanksgiving, present your requests to God. And the peace of God, which transcends all under-standing, will guard your hearts and your minds in Christ Jesus.
- Philippians 4:6, 7

We have set aside a day each year as our National Day of Prayer. While I am excited that we have "officially" established this day to pray and seek God's face, I am a firm believer in the fact that every day should be a day of prayer. Prayer is that intimate, personal connection with the God of the universe, where we openly and honestly praise and worship God with thankfulness and humility, and make our heartfelt petitions known to Him.

And in the quiet and serenity of our praying, God often speaks to us the loudest.

Take time to pray today. Praise Him in the beauty of His holiness, and saturate Heaven with your thanks for His blessings that He showers on those who love Him every day.

Take Him With You:

**Prayer is your intimate connection
to Almighty God. Use it!**

Ron Lambros

A True Gift From God

She is clothed with strength and dignity; she can laugh at the days to come. She speaks with wisdom, and faithful instruction is on her tongue.
Her children arise and call her blessed...
- Proverbs 31:25, 26; 28

A mother is far more than the woman who simply gave you birth. She is an incredibly beautiful example of God's love for each of us—freely given, generous, sacrificial, without limit or end, ever faithful, without compromise, unconditional, and worthy of thanksgiving. Scripture tells us many things about these wonderful women God has given us. *She is noble, priceless, honorable, strong, diligent, generous, caring, compassionate, wise, faithful, praised, and blessed.* (Proverbs 31).

If you have or have had a mother like this, take time to honor and appreciate her today. Thank God for her, and tell her how much you love her and how grateful you are for her. If today is difficult or painful for you, for whatever reason, our loving Father understands your hurt and invites you to reach out to Him for comfort and the healing of your heart.

Finally, if you are a mother today, thank you for your love and sacrifice. You are a true gift from God, and we appreciate you far more than you'll ever know.

Take Him With You:

Mothers are a true gift from God.
Thank Him for yours today.

Ron Lambros

We Remember

Greater love has no one than this:
to lay down one's life for one's friends.
- John 15:13

Today, we remember and honor those who paid the ultimate price while faithfully serving our Country in the Armed Forces. We owe a deep sense of gratitude for these brave men and women who sacrificially gave their lives in defense of our freedom, our liberty, and our peace. We are also indebted to those families who suffered the unimaginable loss of their loved ones who have served and sacrificed their lives for our benefit.

Jesus Himself is our model of sacrifice for good by laying down His very life for us. May each of us thank Him today for those men and women of our Armed Forces who lived and died by His example.

Take Him With You:

Thank God for Jesus
and for all who willingly sacrificed their lives for you.

It Takes a Special Man to Be a Dad!

Children's children are a crown to the aged,
and parents are the pride of their children.
- Proverbs 17:6

The righteous lead blameless lives;
blessed are their children after them.
- Proverbs 20:7

"I will be a Father to you, and you will be my sons and
daughters," says the Lord Almighty.
- II Corinthians 6:18

Father's Day is often a mixed-bag of emotions. For many, it's a warm, joy-filled day of love and appreciation for the man who sacrificed for his family and whose love is unquestioned and unconditional. For others, especially in our culture today, Father's Day holds resentment and bitterness for a man who abandoned his God-given responsibility for his family, either leaving them with painful memories or no memories at all.

The old adage holds true: *Any man can be a father, but it takes a special man to be a dad!* The Scriptures promise that godly fathers leave a godly heritage and legacy, and are blessed beyond measure for generations to come.

But if you are struggling today because of the painful memories the word "father" conjures up, please know that your Heavenly Father knows, cares, and understands, and He waits patiently to fill that void in your heart with a love that has no limits or end.

May you be blessed and filled with joy and thanksgiving today as you celebrate your earthly father AND your Heavenly Father.

Take Him With You:

Any man can be a father,
but it takes a special man to be a dad!

True Freedom

For the wages of sin is death,
but the gift of God is eternal life in Christ Jesus our Lord.
- Romans 6:23

We celebrate with grateful and thankful hearts our freedom as a people and Nation. This priceless gift has been made possible only by the blessing of Almighty God and the sacrifice of so many.

But our truest freedom was provided by Jesus Christ, who died alone for our sin on an inglorious cross on a battlefield called Calvary. There, He conquered death and hell, all to provide us with an abundant and eternal life if we truly believe!

And he whom the Son sets free is free indeed!

Take Him With You:

**Your ultimate freedom was paid
for on the cross of Jesus Christ.**

Ron Lambros

Honor in Labor

Whatever you do, work at it with all your heart,
as working for the Lord, not for human masters...
- Colossians 3:23

There is honor in labor and hard work. God designed work as a way for us to achieve personal success, satisfaction, and fulfillment in our efforts.

Since the beginning of time itself, work has been in existence. God Himself worked for 6 days and then rested. Adam worked diligently in the Garden of Eden. Moses and David were shepherds, and the Apostle Paul was a tentmaker. So it has been for centuries since. Work has always been a part of life.

Today, we pause to honor those who labor and work, providing not only for their families, but also contributing to our society as we know it. Take pride in your work. Work honestly and skillfully. Make your work an altar of praise to God for the gifts He has blessed you with that enable you to be successful. And most of all, give Him glory and honor in all that you do.

Take Him With You:

Make your work an altar of praise
and thanksgiving to God.

An Act of Terrorism

He is the atoning sacrifice for our sins, and not only for ours but also for the sins of the whole world.
- I John 2:2

I would never minimize 9/11 or its effect on our Nation and her people, but we must never forget that the single greatest act of terrorism in the history of all mankind occurred, not in New York City, but on a lonely hill called Golgotha, where Satan hurled all the vile venom and evil in his arsenal at one solitary Man. Yet, a single cross and its lone Occupant remained steadfast and resolute throughout the horrendous ordeal.

In that one single act of incredible personal sacrifice, God assured us all that we could face any sin, any hardship, and any foe and be found loved, victorious, and forgiven!

Hallelujah! What a Savior!

Take Him With You:

**Jesus Christ endured the greatest
act of terrorism the world has ever known.**

Ron Lambros

Deserving of Honor

Be on your guard; stand firm in the faith;
be courageous, be strong.
- I Corinthians 16:13

The Bible instructs us to give honor to those deserving of honor and praise. This is the day we set aside every year to recognize those brave men and women who have served or currently serve in our military. We honor each of you and are indebted to you for your sacrificial service.

Stay the course and fight the good fight. Our freedoms depend on you, your dedication, and the favor of Almighty God.

Take Him With You:

To those who serve or have served in our military, thank you!

It's Biblical!

I will bless those who bless you, and whoever curses you I will curse; and all peoples on earth will be blessed through you.
- Genesis 12:3

On what promises to be one of the most influential and impactful elections of our lifetime, we must consider one incredibly powerful topic among all the rest. True, the sanctity of life and the welfare and status of the family are vastly important, as are economic considerations that affect us all. But as a Nation and people desiring the blessing of God, we must focus our attention on one thing and one thing alone: Israel!

God's Word is very specific. In Genesis 12:3, God speaks directly about Israel and says, "*I will bless those who bless you, and him who dishonors you I will curse, and in you all the families of the earth shall be blessed.*" It does not get plainer than that!

If America is to maintain its blessing and favor from God and be truly considered "one Nation under God," then we *must* elect the candidate that embraces a love for, and commitment to, Israel. Period.

Now, go to the polls and show God that it's not personal and it's not political...it's Biblical!

Take Him With You:

If we honor Israel and support her welfare,
God will bless America.

He Deserves Nothing Less

Let them give thanks to the Lord for his unfailing love and his wonderful deeds for mankind, for he satisfies the thirsty and fills the hungry with good things.
- Psalm 107:8, 9

Many people think that Thanksgiving is a fun day of family, food, and football. While these might have their place in today's culture, it's important to pause and reflect on the true meaning of celebrating this special day. We all know about the Pilgrims and the first Thanksgiving—that this was a day to thank God for the bountiful harvest and the blessings of the preceding year. With each following generation, new traditions and meanings were either added or forgotten. Today, it can begin with the Macy's Thanksgiving Day Parade and finish with Uncle Bob having that last piece of pecan pie, while other adults plan their shopping strategies for Black Friday savings the next day.

Today—*especially today*—we should each pause and reflect on all that God has so graciously blessed us with and thank Him for each one. Begin with your family, the food you'll enjoy, and just being together in a festive spirit.

But then, go deeper. Thank Him for answered and unanswered prayers, your freedoms and peace in our Nation, your health, your job, your home, His faithfulness and promises in the past, and the hope of a bright future. Thank Him for His unconditional love for you. Thank Him for your salvation and the promise of eternal life. Thank Him for the abundant life He promised and that you enjoy every day. I'll bet if you took the time to jot down everything you should thank God for, you would certainly fill up a page or two of items with that list.

You see, it's not the day that matters, it's the *spirit* of the day that counts! May each of us pause today and thank God for His incredible blessing on us individually, as a family, and as a Country. He deserves nothing less!

Take Him With You:

Thank God for all of His blessings in your life, today and every day.

The Twelve Days of Christmas

"Jesus"

In the sixth month of Elizabeth's pregnancy, God sent the angel Gabriel to Nazareth, a town in Galilee, to a virgin pledged to be married to a man named Joseph, a descendent of David. The virgin's name was Mary. The angel went to her and said, "Greetings, you who are highly favored! The Lord is with you."

Mary was greatly troubled at his words and wondered what kind of greeting this might be. But the angel said to her, "Do not be afraid, Mary; you have found favor with God. You will conceive and give birth to a son, and you are to call him Jesus."
- Luke 1:26-31

Mary struggled with the news. Highly favored. Pregnant? Unwed and expecting? What would people think? What would Joseph think? Then she heard it for the first time:

"Jesus!"

The angel's instruction to name her first-born child. She had no way of knowing that this was the only name by which men might be saved. She only knew that in the sovereignty of God, she would obey and call her baby boy, Jesus.

> ## *Take Him With You:*
> You, like Mary, have heard and know His name...Jesus!

She Knew

At that time Mary got ready and hurried to a town in the hill country of Judea, where she entered Zechariah's home and greeted Elizabeth. When Elizabeth heard Mary's greeting, the baby leaped in her womb, and Elizabeth was filled with the Holy Spirit. In a loud voice she exclaimed: "Blessed are you among women, and blessed is the child you will bear!"
- Luke 1:39-42

Mary pondered all that the angel had said to her and quietly accepted God's plan in her heart. But she had to tell someone. Her cousin, Elizabeth, would understand! She, too, was with child.

Making her way through the dusty streets, she came to Elizabeth's door. When Elizabeth heard Mary's voice, she knew. Her own baby, who would one day become John the Baptist, leaped within her womb and began celebrating God's gift, the soon-coming Messiah, Jesus of Nazareth!

Take Him With You:

You, like John, should celebrate the Christ of Christmas.

Ron Lambros

Pregnant By the Holy Ghost

"How will this be," Mary asked the angel, "since I am a virgin?"

The angel answered, "The Holy Spirit will come on you,
and the power of the Most High will overshadow you.
So the holy one to be born will be called the Son of God."
- Luke 1:34, 35

Now came the hardest part of all: Mary had to tell Joseph. She loved the gentle carpenter with every fiber of her being, but would he, could he, believe her? Pregnant by the Holy Ghost?

Taking his cracked and calloused hands into her own, and looking deep into his eyes, she shared all that the angel had told her. Their son would be called, "Jesus", the long-awaited Messiah.

Take Him With You:

Your faith must believe,
even when logic and reason say otherwise.

All My Love, Jesus

Peace in Joseph's Heart

...an angel of the Lord appeared to him in a dream and said, "Joseph, son of David, do not be afraid to take Mary home as your wife, because what is conceived in her is from the Holy Spirit. She will give birth to a son, and you are to give him the name Jesus, because he will save his people from their sins."
- Matthew 1:20, 21

Joseph took all the words that Mary had spoken to him as truth, though his mind found it difficult to fully comprehend.

While tossing and turning in a fitful sleep, the angel spoke peace to Joseph's heart in a dream, confirming all that Mary had said. He was an honorable man and knew what he must do. He would marry Mary, protecting her from the vicious village gossips. He was determined to follow through on God's plan, no matter the personal sacrifice.

Take Him With You:

You will experience God's plan for your life when you yield in obedience to Him.

Ron Lambros

No Ordinary Child

When Joseph woke up, he did what the angel of the Lord had commanded him and took Mary home as his wife. But he did not consummate their marriage until she gave birth to a son. And he gave him the name Jesus.
- Matthew 1:24, 25

The months passed all too quickly. Joseph and Mary would wed and vowed that no sexual intimacy would occur until after the Christ-child was born.

Mary's pregnancy began to show, and Joseph did his best to protect her reputation and his. It was difficult in a culture where a child born out of wedlock could mean death by stoning for the mother. But this was no ordinary child. He was the Messiah, God's gift to the world!

Take Him With You:

Trusting God above all
often means personal sacrifice on your part.

Counting the Days

In those days Caesar Augustus issued a decree that a census should be taken of the entire Roman world. (This was the first census that took place while Quirinius was governor of Syria.) And everyone went to their own town to register.

- Luke 2:1-3

Joseph heard the rumor that a census would be taken and that he and Mary would need to return to his hometown. Counting the days, they also knew that Mary would be very close to her due date when the journey would be taken. Joseph was concerned, but Mary remained strong because she knew that God would do whatever was necessary to complete His miraculous plan. A virgin would soon deliver the Son of God!

Take Him With You:

Your desire for God's plan for your life will only be found through faith.

Ron Lambros

God's Approval

Because Joseph her husband was faithful to the law,
and yet did not want to expose her to public disgrace,
he had in mind to divorce her quietly.
- Matthew 1:19

Joseph and Mary would hear the whispers and see the sly stares everywhere they went. People were beginning to talk. Even the religious leaders in the village were raising eyebrows. But Joseph was determined to protect Mary at all costs and stayed honorable in his promise to her. The baby would often kick and move within her womb. It was God's way of showing His approval for the couple's obedience in all that they did.

Take Him With You:

Your faith often comes at great personal sacrifice, but always honors God.

All My Love, Jesus

Coming Soon!

So Joseph also went up from the town of Nazareth in Galilee to Judea, to Bethlehem the town of David, because he belonged to the house and line of David. He went there to register with Mary, who was pledged to be married to him and was expecting a child.
- Luke 2:4, 5

The road from Nazareth was already crowded when Joseph and Mary left their home for Bethlehem. Halfway through the journey, Joseph looked back and saw that tears had stained the dust that caked on Mary's face. She was in labor. Joseph tugged a bit harder on the young donkey's reins. It wasn't far, but he was concerned. God's Son was coming soon and the masses just walked right by them with nothing more than a passing glance.

Take Him With You:

**Your obedience and God's plan
are often unseen by man, but always by God.**

Ron Lambros

Carried By a Donkey

"For no word from God will ever fail."
"I am the Lord's servant," Mary answered.
"May your word to me be fulfilled." Then the angel left her.
- Luke 1:37, 38

The journey to Bethlehem was taking its toll as Mary's labor intensified. She struggled physically and spiritually. How could this really be happening? In her teens, a virgin, and about to give birth to the Son of God, the long-awaited Messiah, conceived of the Holy Ghost. The Miracle of Christmas was being carried on the back of a lowly donkey because, as Mary knew in her heart, with God, all things are possible.

Take Him With You:

**God often uses the ordinary
to bring about the extraordinary in your life.**

Mary's Only Thoughts

*While they were there,
the time came for the baby to be born...
- Luke 2:6*

Mary sat on a pile of fresh straw, exhausted from the trip to Bethlehem and the unsuccessful search for a room. Her heart pondered all that had happened: the angelic visit, pregnant by the Holy Ghost, telling Elizabeth and Joseph, the looks and the stares, and finally, the census journey. Now, her pangs of labor grew stronger and more regular, but her only thoughts were that she would soon give birth to the Son of God and call His name, Jesus.

The long-awaited Messiah was almost here.

Take Him With You:

Your highest priority should always be spiritually-minded.

Ron Lambros

New Hope

...and she gave birth to her firstborn, a son.
She wrapped him in cloths and placed him in a manger,
because there was no guest room available for them.
- Luke 2:7

Mary's labor ended with the Baby's wail that softly permeated the Bethlehem streets. The prophesies of old had now met with God's promise of Redemption in the birth of the Christ Child. The King had arrived! His throne, a manger. His robe, tattered cloth. His crown, the blood that dried on his head from birth. His first banquet, mother's milk. His first subjects, barnyard animals. All nature announced His presence. The Savior of the world became flesh, and all mankind was given new hope!

Immanuel! God with us! And He is with us still!

Take Him With You:

Always remember that God's perfect plan will always come to pass.

All My Love, Jesus

What the World Needs

And there were shepherds living out in the fields nearby,
keeping watch over their flocks at night.
An angel of the Lord appeared to them, and the glory of the
Lord shone around them, and they were terrified.
But the angel said to them, "Do not be afraid. I bring you good
news that will cause great joy for all the people.
Today in the town of David a Savior has been born to you; he is
the Messiah, the Lord. This will be a sign to you: You will find a
baby wrapped in cloths and lying in a manger."
Suddenly a great company of the heavenly host appeared with
the angel, praising God and saying, "Glory to God in the highest
heaven, and on earth peace to those on whom his favor rests."
- Luke 2:8-14

"For unto you is born this day in the city of David a Savior, which is Christ the Lord." In His purest love and wisdom, God knew what the world needed more than anything. It was not another king, or prophet, or charismatic leader. More than anything else, the world needed a Savior, and we still do.

May you find the contentment and peace of knowing Jesus Christ as Savior and Lord of your life this Christmas. God has given the perfect, eternal gift for anyone to receive by grace and faith.

Merry Christmas!

Take Him With You:

Jesus Christ: God's greatest gift
to the world at Christmas and every day!

All My Love, Jesus

Happy Birthday!

For you created my inmost being;
you knit me together in my mother's womb.
I praise you because I am fearfully and wonderfully made...

- Psalm 139:13, 14

"For I know the plans I have for you," declares the Lord,
"plans to prosper you and not to harm you, plans to give
you hope and a future."

- Jeremiah 29:11

The Lord your God is with you, the Mighty Warrior who saves.
He will take great delight in you; in his love he will no
longer rebuke you, but will rejoice over you with singing.

- Zephaniah 3:17

Happy Birthday! Today is your special day! Embrace this milestone in your life and celebrate it!

Sadly, many look on this day as just another ordinary day. It's just another day to mark off the calendar as we go about our humdrum lives. But God sees it differently. To Him, it's a day to jump and shout and celebrate with the same vim and vigor of the clock striking midnight on New Year's Eve! And why shouldn't He? Why shouldn't you? Look at what God has done to give each of us reason to celebrate this day!

First, God made you just the way you are, and just like Adam and Eve, God sees you as "very good."

Secondly, God has a very special plan and purpose for your life, and has given you all the gifts and talents you need to accomplish them both. Embrace your unique abilities. God is counting on you!

Lastly, you are so special to Him that God not only delights and rejoices in you, but He actually sings over you! I've heard "Happy Birthday to You" sung more times than I care to count, but the thought of God doing the singing is better than any opera or vocal performance I could ever imagine!

So, "Happy Birthday!" God and I both hope you celebrate it well!

Take Him With You:

Today is a special day to God. It's your birthday. Celebrate it!

All My Love, Jesus

My Personal Story and Challenge

However, I consider my life worth nothing to me;
my only aim is to finish the race and
complete the task the Lord Jesus has given me—
the task of testifying to the good news of God's grace.

- Acts 20:24

It has been said that the path on any journey begins with one single step. For me, that step began on April 15, 1977, at 9:42pm, in the old City Coliseum in Jacksonville, Florida. It was at that very moment that the loving pursuit of a God of unimaginable mercy, love, and grace, met the total and complete surrender of my will and I was gloriously saved by giving my heart and life to Jesus Christ. My aimless quest for earthly success and worldly materialism crumbled when it met the passionate Savior who had been quietly working out His plan and purpose for my life when I didn't even know it. I was changed forever!

I cannot fathom all of the hows and whys of God's unconditional love for me that night. I know it began on a cross centuries before, but, "Why me?" I've asked myself that question a thousand times. Why would God choose me, so unworthy and so undeserving, to, one day, lead international broadcast ministries that shared the Gospel of Jesus Christ with millions of people around the world, and to have the joy of traveling around that same world and personally sharing that same Gospel? Why would I be blessed with the honor and privilege of serving with some of the most respected preachers and teachers of the Gospel, and staffs who love and serve God so unselfishly? And why would I be blessed with a family and friends who love and serve God with the same passion as I do, and love me, support me, and pray for me daily? These are questions I'll spend eternity asking. For now, all I can do is say "Thank You!" to a Savior whose nail-pierced hands hold mine every day, and guide me in the ways I should go as I am obedient to follow Him.

I pray that you know this same Savior. If you do, then you, too, know the joy and peace that only comes from personally knowing Jesus. If you don't know Him, you can be as blessed as I am right now by simply taking your first step on the path to Heaven and eternity by praying this simple prayer:

"Dear God, I know that I'm a sinner and I ask for your forgiveness. I believe that Jesus Christ is your Son and I believe that He died on the cross for my sin. I believe that He rose again on the third day and I trust Him as my Savior and want to follow Him as the Lord of my life starting right now. Lead me every day and help me to do your will. Thank you, God, for saving me. Amen."

If you prayed that prayer, I believe with all my heart that you have been saved, born again, and are now going to Heaven. I rejoice with you and would love to hear from you! Please drop me a note and share your story with me. My address is: Ron Lambros, P. O. Box 870924, Stone Mountain, GA 30087. Or, send me an email at:

rlambros@ronlambrosministries.org.

Beginning your journey with God is the most exciting thing you can ever do. Please know that I love you and I'm praying for you!

Devotion Page Index By Topic

115, 118, 128, 158, 160, 172, 179, 183, 192, 193, 205, 206, 207

Temptation

Pages 14, 157, 176

Troubled

Pages 15, 20, 36, 40, 53, 108, 138, 150, 153, 156, 164, 184, 185, 201, 203

Trust

Pages 1, 5, 10, 27, 34, 36, 37, 47, 50, 52, 53, 57, 63,

65, 66, 69, 70, 73, 80, 93, 107, 121, 132, 133, 135, 137, 147, 150, 151, 153, 159, 173, 174, 182, 191, 199, 206, 211

Worry

Pages 31, 85, 150, 172, 174, 191, 203

Scripture Glossary

Old Testament

Genesis

1:1...Page 13

1:31...Page 74

12:3...Page 243

28:15...Page 184

50:20...Page 17

Exodus

4:10-12...Page 145

14:14...Page 189

34:14...Page 54

Numbers

14:18...Page 204

23:19...Page 146

Deuteronomy

7:9...Page 83

11:1...Page 211

31:6...Page 51

31:8...Page 130

Joshua

1:9...Page 46

1st Samuel

16:7...Page 4

1st Kings

3:9...Page 78

Scripture Glossary

New Testament